FOREVER
ALBION

by
David Instone

In Association With The
Birmingham Post & Mail

Thomas Publications

First published in Great Britain in October, 2006, by
Thomas Publications, PO Box 17, Newport,
Shropshire, England, TF10 7WT
www.thomaspublications.co.uk

ISBN 0 9550585 1 1

Printed and bound by Cromwell Press, Trowbridge

Contents

Introduction 4

A Club Is Born .6

Among The Big Prizes 7

Back In The Big Time 11

Cup Kings Once More 14

A Tough Act To Follow 19

Turbulent Times 29

Astle Arrives .34

League Cup Heroics 38

Travelling The World 48

Ashman: Cup Winner 52

Albion In Europe (Part One) 63

Still A Major Force 70

Youth Cup Heroics 77

A Wembley Return 84

Levelling Out .86

The Mauling of Man Utd (Part One) 94

Storm Clouds Gather 99

The Asa Hartford Affair 102

The Giles Revolution 115

Allen's Prize Legacy 123

The Mauling of Man Utd (Part Two) 127

Big Ron, Big Ambitions 130

A Funny Thing Happened 139

End Of A Golden Era 155

Nearly Men Again 159

Albion In Europe (Part Two) 163

On The Slippery Slope 169

Hurtling Downwards 179

Climbing Back In Style 182

Subscribers .188

Introduction

FA Cups, League Cups, European adventures, promotions and relegations, a League Championship triumph......it's easy to see why West Bromwich Albion have been so well served by literature over the years.

As founder members of the Football League, they are steeped in the great traditions of the game; a breeding ground for working-class heroes and local pride.

Life at The Hawthorns has its ups and downs but is rarely dull. Even in the last quarter of a century and a bit, without winning any major silverware, Albion have qualified for the UEFA Cup through their League placing, reached two major cup semi-finals, been relegated four times - once to the third tier of English football - won promotion three times and tasted both the elation and despair that comes with competing in the play-offs.

They have also totally rebuilt their ground and, largely through the early boing-boing days of the 1990s, found a new generation of fans to replace the thousands who went missing in the 1980s.

Older supporters will have recognised the excitement of this return to good health. In 1930-31, Albion became the first club ever to win the FA Cup and promotion in the same season, then they went agonisingly close in 1953-54 to doing what no team had done in the 20th century and win the FA Cup and the top flight in the same season.

Add to all that the magnificent cup-fighting days of the 1960s - highlighted by four major cup final appearances in a five-year spell that also included an FA Cup semi-final defeat and a European Cup Winners Cup quarter-final defeat - the cultured 1970s rebirth under Johnny Giles and then the flamboyant flirtation with greatness under Ron Atkinson soon afterwards, and the Hawthorns tapestry becomes a rich one indeed.

We believe *Forever Albion* will emerge as a quality addition to the bookshelves of Baggies fans and do justice to these memorable deeds. Certainly, we have left no stone unturned in ensuring that those supporters are given material of the highest possible exclusivity.

Without overlooking any of the iconic occasions - FA Cup finals in 1931, 1935, 1954 and 1968, three League Cup finals, Oldham away in 1976, the play-off final in 1993 and the latter-day promotion triumphs - we think we have unearthed hundreds of gems that haven't previously been seen in print. No-one should be looking away in exasperation and complaining that these are just the same old photos wheeled out under a different title.

The Birmingham Post & Mail's handsome picture library has been the source for the vast majority of the content, so we have to thank the many fine photographers from those two titles as well as their counterparts on the Sports Argus and Sunday Mercury, for the work that appears within the 192 pages of this publication.

We are delighted the company have again seen fit to allow us to repeatedly visit their archives and bring into the public domain old treasures that would otherwise have been left gathering dust. We hope the Post & Mail are as happy with the end product as we are and view this book as an underpinning of the strong bond they enjoy with the Baggies and the club's supporters. Indeed, we trust that Albion will be delighted, too, that their exciting exploits over close on 130 years are given a thorough airing in what is effectively a history in pictures.

At the Post & Mail, we pay particular acknowledgement to Adam Fradgley in the photographic department for his encouragement, cooperation and eagerness to see the project through. He and his staff have supported us no end, particularly in finding material from the 'electronic' era of the last 15 years or so, as have the scanners and the personnel of the library itself.

We're also grateful to the promotions department and to BBC Radio WM for joining Albion in publicising the product generously and helping ensure that, as a result, around 220 fans have their names in the special scroll of honour at the back for posterity.

Talking of which, John Homer and the Official West Bromwich Albion Supporters Club have helped well beyond the call of duty; not only with promoting what is arguably the biggest and most exclusive collection of photographs ever published about the club and with assisting in the book's launch, but also, in John's case, with a host of research matters. Laurie Rampling, Tricia Mills and the author's wife, Liz, have also played a big part in bringing this lengthy labour of love to its conclusion.

Around 30,000 words and 375 exclusive photographs appear within these pages. Read and reminisce!

A Club Is Born

Albion quickly made their mark on the football world, winning the FA Cup for the first time by beating Preston's so-called Invincibles in 1888, the year both clubs also became founder members of the Football League. The Baggies defeated Wednesbury Old Athletic, Mitchell's St George, Wolves, Stoke, Old Carthusians and Derby Junction en route for a 2-1 final triumph at The Oval.

Albion press in a 5-3 home win over Reading on January 21, 1928. The club were in Division Two for the first time in 16 years and finished only eighth despite a strong finish. Goals came in rich supply, though, with Jimmy Cookson hitting four here for the second League game running and netting two at Blackpool a week later. Sensationally, he had scored six at home to Blackpool on September 17 and would end the term with 38 League goals.

THE ALBION'S FINE RECORD.

Whilst the Villa have accomplished an unprecedented feat in winning the F.A. Cup six times, West Bromwich Albion have also set up a record in the history of the game. They have won the League with a record number of points, and, with still a game to play at home, should finish up the campaign with an aggregate of 60 points, or six more than Sunderland obtained in the season of 1912-13. What is more, the Albion had surpassed Sunderland's record when they had played in 38 games.

Practically all the honours that Association football offers had been secured by the Albion prior to this season, but they had never won the League, and consequently their success in such a striking and decisive fashion has evoked great enthusiasm, not only at West Bromwich, but also in Birmingham and the district generally, where the splendid consistency of the team has been much admired.

The feat has been accomplished by all-round ability and skill. Pearson, Smith and Pennington have formed a magnificent defence, and the excellent manner in which the last-named has performed throughout the season has been a source not only of general admiration, but also of amazement, for he has been playing for more than 17 years. He has been quite the Pennington of old, and has undoubtedly been the greatest left back in the country.

Richardson, Bowser, and McNeal have been a magnificent half-back line, perhaps unsurpassed by any in the country, whilst collectively and individually the forwards have borne themselves in a gratifying manner, and that effectiveness has not been wanting is shown by the fact that they have scored 100 goals, of which the largest number is claimed by Morris, one of the greatest opportunists in the country. From every point of view it has been a great season for the Albion, whose match at Tottenham on Saturday week will evoke keen interest, and should raise a large sum of money for charitable purposes.

There wasn't such a big fuss in those days..... above: How the press reported in 1920 on what remains Albion's only League Championship triumph.

Among The Big Prizes

Tommy Glidden is greeted by the Duke of Gloucester after Albion's 2-1 Wembley final win over Birmingham on April 25, 1931. W G Richardson, seen behind his skipper, scored both Baggies goals, either side of a Joe Bradford equaliser. It was Albion's third FA Cup triumph, their second (in 1892) having come at the expense of Aston Villa at The Oval. Some 150,000 fans turned out to mark this latest victorious return to the Black Country and match-day was marked by a special blue Sports Argus, the front cover of which (below) made it clear Albion also had League glory to chase. W G netted 228 League and FA Cup goals for the club and 100 in wartime football.

1931 also proved the year Albion won promotion back to the top flight. Five days after their first visit to Wembley, players and officials were suitably attired for a trip to Stoke, where a W G Richardson goal gave them a 1-0 win. It was Albion's final away game of a season that saw them make history as the first club to win promotion and the FA Cup, their return being secured by a 3-2 victory over Charlton.

Albion's FA Cup triumph over Blues was followed by three years of letdown in the competition. They went out at home to Villa in round three in 1932, to Chelsea at the same hurdle in 1934 and, in between, in this fourth-round tie at West Ham after a 2-0 Hawthorns conquest of Liverpool. It was at Upton Park in the League in November, 1931, that W G Richardson had scored four times in five minutes - and all in the first nine minutes!

W G Richardson (left) and Teddy Sandford press in Albion's 2-1 League win at Chelsea in March, 1933. The club finished fourth after their sixth placing in their first year back in the top flight and were on a real high; no-one more so than Richardson, who scored 30 goals.

Wembley countdown 1930s style....almost three-quarters of a century before the term 'WAGs' was dreamed up! Albion players decided domestic routine was the best preparation for a final meeting with Sheffield Wednesday after overcoming Port Vale (2-1), Sheffield United (7-1), Stockport (5-0), Preston (1-0) and Bolton (2-0) in their 1934-35 run. Inside-forward Joe Carter, who played 451 Baggies games and won three England caps, opts for quality reading time in this happy family shot (above). Below: Wally Boyes had a special reason for doing well against the Owls - he was born in Sheffield. And the 5ft 3in left-winger obliged with a goal in Albion's 4-2 defeat.

A family snap-shot in the home of Stan Wood, a Halifax-born winger who starred in the 1931 FA Cup final victory over Birmingham but missed out at the twin towers four years later. He played 280 times for the club, scoring no fewer than 66 goals, and also represented the Football League. Wood was nicknamed 'Splinter' and 'The Singing Winger.'

Albion are denied by Wolves keeper Cyril Sidlow in a Molineux meeting of the clubs in the long years of wartime football. This wintry clash was one of many between the clubs during the hostilities, Albion losing in a two-leg Wartime League Cup semi-final in 1941-42. The Baggies had their say, though, when they won the Midland Cup in 1943-44. Such was the impact on careers that centre-half Billy Gripton played more wartime games for Albion than any other player (194) but turned out only 16 times for them in the Football League.

Back In The Big Time

Skipper Jack Vernon stands over a prostrate Jim Sanders after a late Eric Day equaliser pegged Albion back in the big Division Two promotion showdown at Southampton on April 23, 1949. The 30,856 crowd, with thousands locked out, was a Dell League record that stood for 20 years. Arthur Smith scored for the Baggies in a 1-1 draw and Jack Smith's side secured runners-up spot behind Fulham by winning handsomely at Leicester a fortnight later as the Saints fell away. Only a last-day defeat at Grimsby denied Albion the title.

Derby-day trouble brews for Albion as Colin Gibson defeats Jack Vernon's challenge and scores the second of the goals by which Aston Villa won 2-1 at The Hawthorns on December 1, 1951. Ronnie Allen netted for Albion. Vernon, a masterly centre-half, cost a club record £9,500 when recruited from his home city of Belfast in 1947 and won more than 20 senior international caps on the other side of the Irish Sea as well as captaining the long defunct United Kingdom side.

Norman Heath finds himself under pressure from Jack Stamps in Albion's 1-0 home victory over Derby on April 12, 1952. Ronnie Allen scored the decider in the second of what proved to be four straight wins for the club and, by following up with a hat-trick at Wolves three days later, was on his way to a final League haul for the season of 32 goals. Albion finished in a modest 13th spot - their third successive mid-table placing. Also visible through the netting is defender Stan Rickaby.

Jack Vernon says his farewells prior to returning to his native Ireland in 1952. By now in his early 30s, Vernon had scored only once in exactly 200 senior Baggies appearances - the deciding goal at home to Sheffield Wednesday on Christmas Day in 1948 - but was a hugely popular figure. On the other end of the warm hand-shake is Joe Kennedy while (from the left) are coach W G Richardson, the trainer Arthur Fitton and team-mates Ronnie Allen and Norman Heath.

Ronnie Allen is pictured in full devastating flight on his way to a Hawthorns hat-trick in the 4-0 thrashing of Huddersfield on October 10, 1953. It was one of ten times the brilliant forward scored three or more goals in one game for the club, another of those occasions coming at home to Chelsea only a fortnight later. Albion had sensationally won 7-3 at Newcastle in September, 1953, and would soon embark on a run of five successive victories that included the 5-2 eclipse of Chelsea.

A challenge by defender Lionel Smith shuts out Ronnie Allen during an Arsenal visit to The Hawthorns in the 1950s. Keeper Jack Kelsey is no doubt a relieved man - and was entitled to be. The Gunners were beaten on six League trips out of six to the ground, starting in 1950-51, although their stock was high enough at the time for them to win the FA Cup in 1950 and the League Championship in 1953. Allen scored 27 top-flight goals in 1953-54 but was still not the club's top League marksman. That honour went to Johnny Nicholls (28).

Cup Kings Once More

A shock in the making as left-back Len Millard and centre-half Jimmy Dugdale fail to prevent Port Vale taking the lead through Albert Leake in the 1954 FA Cup semi-final at Villa Park. Albion had earlier beaten Chelsea, Rotherham, Newcastle and Tottenham but found the Third Division side a real handful until goals came from Jimmy Dudley and former Vale man Ronnie Allen (penalty).

Albion fans are in good heart and in suitable attire, rattles, hats and all, as they prepare for the club's first visit to Wembley for virtually two decades.

May the best team win - as long as it's us! Albion skipper Len Millard (left) and genial Preston captain and forward Tom Finney use one hand to hold the FA Cup and the other to extend a friendly greeting as they meet at a TV studio a few days before the Wembley showdown between their sides in 1954. Finney, capped 76 times by England and widely regarded as one of the nation's finest footballers, had a surprisingly poor game in the final.

Two views of the Ronnie Allen goal that opened the scoring mid-way through the first half of Albion's ninth appearance in an FA Cup final. Above: Left-winger George Lee, with Johnny Nicholls in support, unhinges the Preston defence and supplies the ball across goal for Ronnie Allen (bottom picture) to rush in and glide home. The stricken keeper is George Thompson but his side recovered well and were soon to equalise through a header by Angus Morrison - and then take a 2-1 lead through an offside-looking Charlie Wayman goal.

A less seen view of one of Wembley's most famous goals. This Ronnie Allen penalty is most frequently portrayed from a shot taken by a camera at the opposite end of the stadium, complete with the sight of Albion keeper Jim Sanders cowering by his post, unable to look. But here is a though-the-net view of the goal that made it 2-2 well into the second half. It was Allen's 34th and last goal of a tremendous season in which Johnny Nicholls had netted 32 in all competitions. Frank Griffin struck the Wembley winner with only three minutes left.

Celebration time for Albion players and their womenfolk at West Bromwich Town Hall following the club's winning of the FA Cup for the fourth time. Frank Griffin is pictured just right of centre in a striped tie, his goal in the dying minutes having proved the difference in a thrilling final. Albion would have had more silverware to show from the season had they not been overhauled by Wolves and left as runners-up in a memorable all-West Midlands race for the League Championship title.

Didn't we do well? Len Millard swaps the FA Cup for two-year-old son Stanley during the festivities back in the Black Country. Also pictured are the captain's wife and the wife of chairman Major Wilson Keys. Millard, a Coseley-born left-back who started out in life as a centre-forward, is Albion's all-time second highest appearance maker behind Tony Brown after playing 627 games for them. He missed only 13 matches in ten seasons from 1946-47.

One of the skipper's duties…..Len Millard, proudly attired in his club blazer, takes to the microphone to say the necessary post-final thank-yous on behalf of his victorious team.

The atmosphere is a little less formal as Ray Barlow shows off the spoils of the club's success during a visit to Blackheath, near Dudley, with many excited youngsters eager to get a close-up view.

Ray Barlow funnels back to help out his defence during the First Division derby at Wolves on October 23, 1954. And so he might. The clash between the League champions and the FA Cup winners went all one way with a 4-0 home victory less than a month after the clubs had fought out a magnificent 4-4 Charity Shield draw at Molineux. Ronnie Allen scored a hat-trick in that epic and was to finish as the leading First Division scorer that season with 27 goals.

A Tough Act To Follow

Doing their bit for the community are Jim Sanders (left), Ronnie Allen (seated) and Len Millard, who played a staggering 1,474 Albion games between them and stayed long after FA Cup glory, although 17th place in 1954-55 was a disappointing finish for the side after all the heroics of the year before. Albion's reign as Cup holders ended in a 4-2 fourth-round defeat at home to Charlton.

The masterful Ray Barlow in action again, this time during the 1956-57 campaign, in which Albion finished in between Aston Villa and Birmingham flush in the middle of the First Division. And the left-half, capped once by England, featured superbly amid a strong West Midlands influence in the FA Cup semi-finals, with Albion unlucky to be held to a Molineux draw by Villa and then beaten by them by the only goal in the replay at St Andrew's.

An unusual view of The Hawthorns captured in September, 1957, with Albion's newly installed £18,000 floodlights the main focus. The club's first game under the lights was the top-flight match at home to Chelsea in the middle of that month, although the official opening was at a friendly against the Moscow team CDKA. The picture is taken in the direction of the Smethwick End, with Halfords Lane disappearing into the distance.

Ronnie Allen evades Bolton keeper Eddie Hopkinson during the 2-2 Hawthorns draw on October 12, 1957. The two were England internationals as well as club rivals and Allen, who would score the last of his 234 Albion goals against the same opponents in February, 1961, had the last laugh in this game by netting a penalty. Less than a month earlier, the Baggies had slammed Manchester City 9-2 during a fine start to the season, Frank Griffin scoring a hat-trick.

A TOUGH ACT TO FOLLOW

Joe Kennedy climbs above Bobby Charlton to head clear in Albion's thrilling 4-3 victory over Manchester United on October 26, 1957 - one of the defender's 397 games for the club. Less than four months later, Charlton survived the Munich air crash, soon after which the teams met three more times, with Albion winning 4-0 in the League at Old Trafford but going out of the FA Cup there 1-0 in a quarter-final replay following a 2-2 draw at The Hawthorns.

Ronnie Allen gives Leicester defender Colin Appleton a close-up of the awesome shooting power that wrote his name indelibly into Hawthorns folklore in the 1950s. Potteries-born Allen, later to have two spells as the club's manager, was Albion's highest-ever League scorer with 208 goals until Tony Brown overtook him almost 20 years later - and was harshly represented by the winning of only five England caps.

Ray Barlow and a more distant Stuart Williams watch Clive Jackman keep Tottenham centre-forward Bobby Smith at bay at The Hawthorns on April 7, 1958. The teams had drawn 0-0 at White Hart Lane three days earlier and Albion squeezed in a narrow defeat at Aston Villa before their hopes in this return were hit by the loss of right winger Jimmy Campbell with a fractured leg after only ten minutes. Spurs won 2-0 but Albion still finished fourth in the table.

Tribute is paid to W G Richardson before the clash with Manchester City on March 31, 1959. Albion marked the Hawthorns great's passing with a 3-0 victory the day after winning 2-0 at Maine Road. From left: Derek Hogg, Ray Potter, Don Howe, Maurice Setters, Jimmy Dudley, Derek Kevan, Ronnie Allen, mascot Johnny Tromans, Joe Kennedy, Dave Burnside, Jimmy Campbell, Stuart Williams. Manager Vic Buckingham joined Ajax soon after, his last game seeing Albion relegate Villa via a 1-1 derby draw.

Alec Jackson races goalwards in a 5-0 humiliation of Leicester on September 5, 1959. The Tipton-born forward scored 52 goals in 208 Albion games and netted in this second home win of the season, Albion having sent Manchester United packing 3-2 on kick-off day. The Leicester trio in pursuit are (from left) Tony Knapp, Ken Leek and Len Chalmers. Jackson scored the only goal when Albion completed the double at Filbert Street in the January.

Happy days for the Williamses as they train together after being called up for Wales' game against Ireland at Wrexham in the spring of 1960. The 3-2 home win was the first of 26 senior caps for Graham (left) and came four days after his 22nd birthday while Stuart was already established as skipper in the other full-back position and on his way to a haul of 43 international appearances.

FOREVER ALBION

Dizzy late-season days for Albion as they stride to a 3-1 home win over Sheffield Wednesday on April 16, 1960. With keeper Jock Wallace dealing here with a keen challenge from Johnny Fantham, they were registering a third successive League victory and made it four only two days later when they swamped Birmingham 7-1 at St Andrew's. It all put the seal on an impressive first season under new manager Gordon Clark, with a final placing of fourth.

Autograph hunter's dream. Albion's players are easy prey for this young admirer as they stride out for training in July, 1960. Leading the way are Bobby Robson and Stuart Williams, with Jock Wallace and Ray Potter behind, followed by Derek Hogg. Bouncing the ball half-way back in the group is a young Bobby Hope, who had made his debut as a 16-year-old in a victory against Arsenal in the last game of the previous season.

Ronnie Allen, nearing the end of his Hawthorns playing career before joining Crystal Palace, cuts inside Fulham's George Cohen in Albion's shocking start to 1960-61. The Londoners' 4-2 win at The Hawthorns was Albion's third defeat in three games and the run stretched to five before being sensationally broken by a 6-0 thrashing of Newcastle. Two more losses then followed before the Baggies won two in a row, the second by 6-3 against Manchester City!

David Burnside crashes a shot goalwards during the Baggies' Hawthorns clash with West Ham on October 15, 1960. This one didn't go in but Bobby Robson scored the goal that brought the side a second successive victory after they had triumphed at Bolton seven days earlier. Alas, Gordon Clark's team didn't win any of their next seven matches, the last of which was a 7-1 hammering at Chelsea.

Keith Smith is out of luck with a header in Albion's 4-0 Hawthorns trouncing of Blackburn on November 4, 1961. The Derbyshire-born forward netted twice to help his side end a run of five draws, the last of them a 4-4 thriller at Nottingham Forest in which he was also on target. Derek Kevan (left) and Alec Jackson scored Albion's other goals against Rovers, Jackson going on to snatch the point-saver at Ewood Park later in the season.

Albion players surround a wireless on a Ford Anglia to hear they have drawn holders Tottenham at home in round five of the 1961-62 FA Cup. Pictured (from left) in the wake of a 2-1 fourth-round win at Wolves are coach Wilf Dixon, Bobby Robson, Don Howe, Dave Burnside, Stuart Williams, Stan Jones, Clive Clark, Alec Jackson, Keith Smith and Derek Kevan. Spurs won the tie 4-2 and retained the Cup. Picture by courtesy of Associated Newspapers.

All smiles from Albion's players despite their appearance in short sleeves on a crisp winter's morning at The Hawthorns in the early 1960s! Pictured with manager Gordon Clark (back row far left) and trainer Dick Graham are (back row, from left) Stuart Williams, Chuck Drury, Don Howe, Jock Wallace, Joe Kennedy, Bobby Robson, Graham Williams. Front: Brian Whitehouse, Alec Jackson, Dave Burnside, Ronnie Allen, Derek Kevan, Derek Hogg.

Albion's Don Howe (left), Derek Kevan (centre) and Bobby Robson celebrate their call-up by England to the 1962 World Cup in Chile. Kevan was selected as a reserve and none of the trio featured in a side who exited the tournament against eventual winners Brazil in the quarter-final. Robson, who won 20 caps, had Howe as one of his coaches during his spell as national manager more than 20 years later.

Don Howe and keeper Tony Millington watch Graham Williams trying to clear from Derek Dougan at Villa Park on October 6, 1962 - a 2-0 home victory in which Clive Clark and Villa winger Harry Burrows were sent off. They were mixed times for Albion, who had scored six at home to Fulham and five against Bolton while also losing four games early in the season. Burrows played a big part in this clash as he scored the second goal from the penalty spot.

Who are they trying to kid? Short-sleeved Sheffield Wednesday players contrast with opponents who opt for knee pads in this clash in the big freeze of 1963. So severe was it that this January 12 fixture was one of only five played on the worst day for postponements in English and Scottish history. It was the only League game Albion played between December 15 and March 2 - and they lost it 3-0. Second from left as Ronnie Fenton heads goalwards, watched by Derek Kevan, is Gary Megson's father Don.

Turbulent Times

Ray Fairfax clears in a manic start to Jimmy Hagan's managerial reign at The Hawthorns. The full-back, watched by Stan Jones and keeper Ray Potter, could not stop Arsenal winning 2-1 on April 15, 1963 and so complete an Easter double over the Baggies, who lost in between at Blackburn in an unkind run of three games in four days. Hagan had succeeded Archie Macaulay.

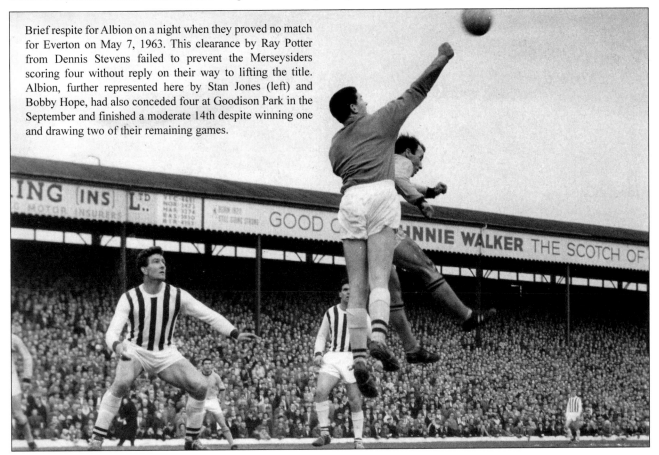

Brief respite for Albion on a night when they proved no match for Everton on May 7, 1963. This clearance by Ray Potter from Dennis Stevens failed to prevent the Merseysiders scoring four without reply on their way to lifting the title. Albion, further represented here by Stan Jones (left) and Bobby Hope, had also conceded four at Goodison Park in the September and finished a moderate 14th despite winning one and drawing two of their remaining games.

Familiar face in unfamiliar colours......John Talbut (right) in action for Burnley in a 0-0 Hawthorns draw on September 21, 1963. Albion had trounced Arsenal 4-0, Fulham 3-0 and Birmingham 3-1 in their previous three home games but were checked by the 1959-60 League champions despite a Clive Clark advance that had keeper Adam Blacklaw discomforted. Clark and the debutant Tony Brown scored in a 2-1 win at Ipswich seven days later while Talbut joined Albion just before Christmas in 1966.

Easy does it! Captain Don Howe shows a delicate touch in helping with lunch at a new steak bar at the Hawthorns Hotel in October, 1963. It proved to be a wholesome preparation for Albion, who won 4-3 the next day at home to Aston Villa, with goals by Bobby Cram, Alec Jackson, Tony Brown and Ken Foggo. Bomber's strike was his first at the ground in senior football.

The trials and tribulations of Hawthorns life under the disciplinarian ways of Jimmy Hagan.
Above: Albion players convene for a showdown meeting with their manager in late 1963 - the
Arctic winter in which they went on strike in protest at being told they couldn't wear tracksuit
bottoms to warm up before training. Gathering their thoughts before the confrontation are
(from left) Stan Jones, Doug Fraser, Graham Williams, skipper Don Howe, Ray Potter, John
Kaye and Terry Simpson. A compromise was eventually reached with the board's intervention.
Below: Hagan's car lies in ruins in the canal after he had hit the wrong pedal and plunged 40
feet down a steep bank as he tried to drive away from the club's Spring Road training ground.
The quick thinking of his players hauled the manager away from a probable icy death but he
didn't go overboard in his thanks as four of them carried him away on a stretcher for treatment
and the start of several weeks away from his desk. Noticing that one of them, keeper Tony
Millington, was out of breath, he said from his vulnerable position: "Millington, you're not fit.
Extra training this afternoon!" No wonder there were some powerful headlines.....

A REVOLT

By BILL HOLDEN

TWENTY-FOUR hours before the English Soccer season
kicks off, West Bromwich Albion players are "on the
verge of revolt" against manager Jimmy Hagan.

'Manager told us to run off and find five kinds of leaves,' say players

Ray Potter winces as he goes down to gather among the flying boots in Albion's excellent 2-0 win at Tottenham on December 28, 1963. The sides had drawn 4-4 in a thriller at The Hawthorns only two days before and this was Albion's third successive away victory. Stan Jones is the no 5, with Don Howe (left) and Doug Fraser the team-mates also in attendance.

Don Howe looks on as Ray Potter produces a decisive punch to deny Alan Deakin in Albion's 1-0 First Division defeat at Aston Villa on February 22, 1964. The Baggies were derby top dogs a week later, though, when they beat Wolves 3-1 at The Hawthorns and finished in a healthy mid-table position - comfortably the highest of a West Midlands quartet completed by Birmingham.

Nottingham Forest duo Henry Newton and John Barnwell see Clive Clark threaten with a header in Albion's 3-2 defeat on April 11, 1964. From left, Alec Jackson, Doug Fraser and Don Howe are the other home players. Howe, who won 23 England caps, all consecutively, was playing the last of his 379 Albion games before joining Arsenal while this also proved to be Jackson's farewell prior to signing for Birmingham. One of Forest's goals came from Colin Addison, who was later to serve as Hawthorns assistant boss.

Not a great one for black and white TV! John Ritchie climbs above Graham Williams in a 5-3 Albion home victory over Stoke that maintained the club's unbeaten start to the seven-game-old 1964-65 season. It was more a day for defenders than forwards. Bobby Cram, uncle of athlete Steve Cram, performed the extremely rare feat of scoring a hat-trick from right-back, two of the three coming from penalties.

Astle Arrives

The first of the 174…..a beaming Jeff Astle is congratulated by Geoff Carter after opening his Albion tally on his home debut against Wolves in October, 1964. The forward, signed for £25,000 from Notts County a week and a half earlier, scored twice, as did John Kaye, in this 5-1 thrashing. Wolves, in the form of Stan Cullis, had also watched Astle, whose heroics were too much for no 2 George Showell, keeper Fred Davies and the grounded Graham Hawkins.

More derby success for Albion as they hold firm to keep out Tony Hateley en route for a 1-0 victory at Villa Park on October 17, 1964. No 5 Stan Jones (left) and keeper Roy Potter are the covering defenders in a game which made it two wins over West Midlands opponents on successive Saturdays. The feat was secured by a Gerry Howshall goal and despite the sending-off of skipper Graham Williams after a clash with Hateley.

Jeff Astle watches his header fly past Colin Withers for one of Albion's goals in their 3-1 home victory over Villa on February 27, 1965. Ken Foggo and visiting duo Charlie Aitken and Lew Chatterley also look on during a contest in which Bobby Cram (penalty) and Bobby Hope netted the winners' other goals. It was a third success in four League games for Albion, who built spectacularly on it by hammering Leicester 6-0 in their Hawthorns fortress next time out, Astle scoring two more.

Take aim, fire! Jeff Astle drills past Gerry Young for the goal that completed his first Albion hat-trick. It came in the 4-2 Hawthorns win over Sheffield Wednesday in early September, 1965, when he was still wearing the no 8 shirt. He and the side ran amok that autumn, leading the table for the first time since 1954 in the process. Astle netted another treble, at Northampton, the following Friday night, having also scored in a midweek 3-2 victory at Everton.

FOREVER ALBION

A famous face in the Hawthorns spotlight....that's Terry Venables (left) in the colours of a Chelsea side on their way to a 2-1 win on October 2, 1965. The midfielder is being watched by Graham Lovett, who made his debut in the corresponding fixture the previous season. Albion's scorer Doug Fraser is the player in the distance as Jeff Astle's legendary prowess in the air overcomes a challenge from Marvin Hinton.

Albion's highly promising 1965-66 campaign continued with a 1-1 draw at Aston Villa (below), where Jeff Astle was on target at a stadium under partial reconstruction ready for England's hosting of the 1966 World Cup finals. Here, Rick Sheppard, early in a two-month run in the senior goalkeeper jersey, produces a safe catch to deny no 8 Willie Hamilton under the watchful eye of Doug Fraser (left) and Graham Lovett.

John Kaye runs away in celebration of his goal in Albion's stunning home win over FA Cup holders Liverpool on October 23, 1965. It was the Baggies' third goal - much to the dismay of defenders Gerry Byrne and Ron Yeats and forward Ian St John - and there was to be no reply. Liverpool lifted the League title in 1965-66 but with no help from Albion, who also drew 2-2 with them at Anfield after memorably winning 3-0 there the previous spring.

Jeff Astle watches a shot bounce wide in Albion's 2-1 win over Peterborough in the first leg of the League Cup semi-final in December, 1965. Jimmy Hagan's side had scored three against Walsall, four at Leeds, six at home to Coventry and three against Villa in a goal-laden run to the last four but needed Tony Brown's second-leg hat-trick at London Road to reach the final 6-3 on aggregate.

League Cup Heroics

Albion reached the League Cup final at their first attempt in 1965-66, never having played in the competition before. It was the last season the cup was concluded over two legs and the outcome hung in the balance after a 2-1 West Ham win at a ground where Albion had lost 6-1 and 4-0 in their previous two visits. Graham Williams, watched by debutant centre-half Danny Campbell and keeper Ray Potter, is on the line above while Martin Peters and Bobby Moore are the home players. Picture courtesy of Associated Newspapers.

No need to worry! West Ham might have been European Cup Winners Cup holders and 1964 FA Cup winners but were destroyed by a magnificent first-half Albion performance in the return - an onslaught described by several of Jimmy Hagan's players as the best team display they ever figured in. It was 4-0 after 34 minutes thanks to John Kaye, Tony Brown, Clive Clark and Graham Williams, with Peters' second-half goal too little too late for the shellshocked Hammers. Kaye is pictured here scoring, with Brown and Clark in support.

LEAGUE CUP HEROICS

Field of dreams. An unusual view of The Hawthorns taken in the month of England's 1966 World Cup triumph. Parts of the landscape have changed since this picture from above during a pre-season practice game more than 40 years ago, most notably the stands. The Birmingham Road End was rebuilt in 1968 and 1993, the Halfords Lane Stand followed suit over a decade later and the Rainbow Stand (now the East Stand) and Smethwick End disappeared in the bulldozer's path in the 1990s.

History made….Clive Clark signals his delight at the goal by Dick Krzywicki that steadied Albion's hold on the League Cup - the first time a Baggies substitute had gone on and scored. Despite a 6-1 thrashing of Villa at the first hurdle, Albion were wobbling at home to newly-promoted Manchester City until Krzywicki, a number-less replacement for Doug Fraser, equalised. Then Clark and the debutant Kenny Stephens secured a 4-2 win.

Albion were locked in a survival fight by the time they crashed to this 3-0 defeat at home to Manchester City on December 10, 1966. Despite their cup heroics, the club had lost five times in six League games and were one place off the bottom of the table. There's all-out effort from Manchester-bred Tony Brown in this picture as he hurls himself full-length at a right-wing cross, supported by winger Clive Clark. But keeper Alan Ogley and his defenders survived. Alan Oakes is the man immediately behind Brown.

Graham Williams welcomes John Talbut after the Burnley centre-half completed a £33,000 move to Albion in December, 1966. Talbut's first game was a 3-0 Boxing Day victory at home to Tottenham - only the club's second League clean sheet of a troubled season. The match, highlighted by a Tony Brown hat-trick and followed by a 0-0 draw between the sides at White Hart Lane 24 hours later, also provided Dennis Clarke with a debut. Completing the line-up are (from left) Bobby Cram, Ray Potter, Doug Fraser and Gerry Howshall.

Albion were certainly not the semi-final opponents West Ham would have chosen for themselves in the 1966-67 League Cup. Memories of their hammering in the 1966 final were still fresh - and no doubt further revived after only 50 seconds of the first leg at The Hawthorns. A centre by Ian Collard provided the opening and Jeff Astle (pictured above in the distance) headed home just inside the far post. Clive Clark looks on from near the penalty spot at a goal that lit the touchpaper and had Tony Brown yelling his delight. Bobby Cram went close with a shot (below) that Jim Standen dived to push wide, with John Kaye and Astle hovering, then just after the quarter-hour, Albion, who had scored a total of 11 times in their previous three home matches against the Hammers, were two up thanks to Clark - the left-winger's fifth goal in that season's competition and one that maintained his record of scoring in every round.

Jeff Astle arrows a low left-foot drive through a cluster of defenders and beyond keeper Jim Standen - also a Worcestershire cricketer - to complete a first-half hat-trick in the League Cup semi-final first leg. The striker's heroics gave Albion a 4-0 lead and that's how the score remained despite chances at both ends in the second half. As a result, Jimmy Hagan's men had rattled in no fewer than 19 goals in only five matches in that season's competition.

A packed Birmingham Road End was a good place to be in the middle and late 1960s! A sixth-place top-flight finish in 1965-66, League Cup glory in the same season, a journey to Wembley in the competition 12 months later and then, of course, a more lucrative prize still in 1967-68. With domestic success, of course, came European qualification twice in the decade, which, coupled with England's World Cup triumph, seemed a good enough reason for excited fans to go searching for those Union Jacks.

Tony Brown worries West Ham's defence and, in particular, Eddie Bovington as the semi-final spotlight switches to Upton Park for the second leg. John Kaye (left) and Clive Clark are up in support.

Brown again tries his luck, this time with a shot, on a night when the loss of an injured and unwell Jeff Astle just before kick-off might have dented Albion's chances. England forwards Johnny Byrne and Geoff Hurst twice gave the Londoners the lead in the first half but Bobby Hope came up with the first equaliser and, just past the hour, Clive Clark's goal silenced a capacity crowd and killed the tie off.

A job well done - Albion's players toast their success in reaching Wembley for the first time in 13 years after seeing off 'World Cup West Ham' by the convincing aggregate score of 6-2. The drinks soon came out in the visitors' dressing room, with a clearly dazed Jeff Astle trying to join in the celebrations (above). Below: Bath-time for (from left) Clive Clark, Ken Foggo (sitting up), Bobby Hope, Graham Williams, Bobby Cram, Ian Collard, John Kaye and Rick Sheppard.

The best-laid plans.....there's no mistaking Albion's determination to hang on to the League Cup as they set off for their Wembley hideaway before the final against Third Division QPR, the shock 7-2 semi-final conquerors of Birmingham on aggregate, in the first weekend of March, 1967. Skipper Graham Williams is determined the silverware is leaving the Black Country only temporarily and appears to have the approval of his team-mates.

And the sickening reality.....right, Clive Clark vacates a scene of utter dejection and rushes away with his loser's tankard after Albion's 3-2 defeat.

It's the final indignity in Albion's Wembley throwaway as QPR defender Ron Hunt goes in hard on keeper Rick Sheppard in the race for possession. Despite the covering of John Kaye (left), the ball broke loose and Mark Lazarus tucked away the winner, much to the consternation of red-shirted Albion players, who made it clear they thought their keeper had been fouled in the build-up. The goal stood, though, and the holders had lost - despite being 2-0 up through former Rangers winger Clive Clark's brace with only 28 minutes to go.

Albion reacted to Wembley pain with a thrilling surge out of relegation danger. Bottom but one entering Easter, they beat Southampton 3-2 at home despite a Tony Brown penalty miss and this scare caused by Terry Paine among Ray Fairfax, Eddie Colquhoun, Graham Williams and John Osborne. Albion won eight and drew one of their last ten games to finish 13th, ten points ahead of doomed Villa.

The Great Escape 1967 style did not save Jimmy Hagan. With survival ensured two games from the end of the season, the axe fell on the manager and word was passed on by chairman Jim Gaunt to (from left) Tony Brown, Ian Collard, Eddie Colquhoun, Doug Fraser, Rick Sheppard, Stan Jones, John Talbut and skipper Graham Williams before the trip to Blackpool, who were already relegated following 30 successive seasons in the top flight.

Travelling The World

All smiles from the Albion party as they depart The Hawthorns for a pre-season tour to Holland under Jimmy Hagan in August, 1964 - a trip that saw them lose 2-1 to Alkmaar, beat ADO 2-1 in The Hague and defeat Ajax 1-0 thanks to a Bobby Hope goal. Long-serving secretary Alan Everiss is taking the photograph while nearest to him is Tommy Glidden, a man who served the club for more than 50 years, as a player, coach, shareholder and director.

Looking relaxed during the formalities before kick-off against Alkmaar on August 8, 1964, are (from left) Terry Simpson, skipper Graham Williams, a half-hidden Stan Jones, Ronnie Fenton, Doug Fraser, Ken Foggo, John Kaye, Bobby Hope, Clive Clark and (behind) Bobby Cram. Albion lost narrowly despite a Clark goal but came back to win the other two games of their Dutch tour, Tony Brown and Doug Fraser netting next time out against ADO.

Heading for the Big Apple.....Albion players prove that life as top-flight footballers is a guaranteed ticket to see the world as they head for New York for a lengthy pre-season tournament in July, 1965. In stifling temperatures, the club played six matches in their four-team group, beating Kilmarnock 2-0, drawing with Ferencvaros of Hungary (1-1) and Polish club Polonia Bytom (2-2) and also losing to all of the same opponents - 2-0, 2-1 and 6-0 respectively.

Graham Williams, Doug Fraser, John Kaye and Ray Potter sample the high life in New York as they look out from the Empire State Building. The trip did no damage to Albion's well-being as preparation for 1965-66. The club won seven of their first ten games in the League and League Cup and led the table in September. Kaye played 361 senior games for Albion, one more than Williams, with Fraser not far behind on 325 and Potter appearing 238 times.

This time South America is the destination in May, 1966, as League Cup holders Albion embark on a six-match end-of-season tour that brought them two victories in Peru, a draw and a defeat in Uruguay, a draw in Argentina and a 2-1 win over Flamengo at the Maracana Stadium in Rio de Janeiro, Brazil, where goals came from Bobby Cram (penalty) and John Kaye. Chairman Jim Gaunt is at the front in the light suit, alongside manager Jimmy Hagan.

Graham Williams, Ray Wilson and coach Albert McPherson are pictured while sightseeing on their travels in South America. Albion and foreign opponents haven't always got on too well over the years and this four-week-long 1966 expedition proved an unhappy one for young midfielder Graham Lovett, who was sent off in both the 1-1 draw against a Uruguayan select X1 in Montevideo and the clash with Flamengo in Rio a fortnight later.

Young centre-half Ron Potter, FA Cup final substitute Dennis Clarke and keeper John Osborne are joined by a youngster as they watch from the bench during Albion's six-game tour of East Africa straight after their Wembley success over Everton. Further along on the touchline are coach Stuart Williams and manager Alan Ashman. The club remained unbeaten in an at times stormy journey through Tanzania, Uganda and Kenya, winning three matches and drawing three.

Far East, 1978, and, under a famous gaze, Albion's players stride out on their ground-breaking tour of China and Hong Kong. The ambitious end-of-season trip made them the first British team to visit the People's Republic and was so innovative that a special BBC2 documentary team were sent to follow them. From left, Mick Martin, Brendon Batson, Tony Brown, Alistair Brown and Cyrille Regis are in the spotlight here. Ron Atkinson's team won all of their five games.

Ashman: Cup Winner

John Kaye became Albion's first substitute to score a League goal when he put this emphatic finishing touch to a 4-1 home win over newly-promoted Wolves on August 30, 1967. Kaye joined Clive Clark, Kenny Stephens and the also pictured Jeff Astle on target, having netted as well in a stormy 3-3 draw at Molineux a week earlier, when a side now managed by Alan Ashman scored twice in the last three minutes. In charge of Wolves was Hawthorns legend Ronnie Allen while Wanderers' keeper was West Bromwich-born Phil Parkes.

No way through for Albion in a goalless deadlock at home to Leicester on October 28, 1967. Even the apparent difficulty Peter Shilton had in the presence of his team-mate John Sjoberg and danger-man Jeff Astle could not bring about a goal for the inconsistent Baggies. It came spectacularly right two weeks later, though, with an 8-1 humiliation of Burnley - one of the club's most handsome victories.

Albion had the happiest of Christmases in 1967 as they pulled off an outstanding double against a Manchester City side destined to win the League Championship. On Boxing Day (above), they won 3-2 in a Hawthorns thriller against Joe Mercer's side, this crashing shot by the two-goal Tony Brown between Tony Book and no 3 Glyn Pardoe helping condemn the club 'Bomber' had shunned six years later in favour of an apprenticeship at The Hawthorns. Four days later (below), Albion were at it again as they won 2-0 at Maine Road through goals by Dick Krzywicki and Brown despite having to survive this near miss which had John Osborne, John Talbut and John Kaye thanking their lucky stars and Doug Fraser handing out a consoling pat on the head.

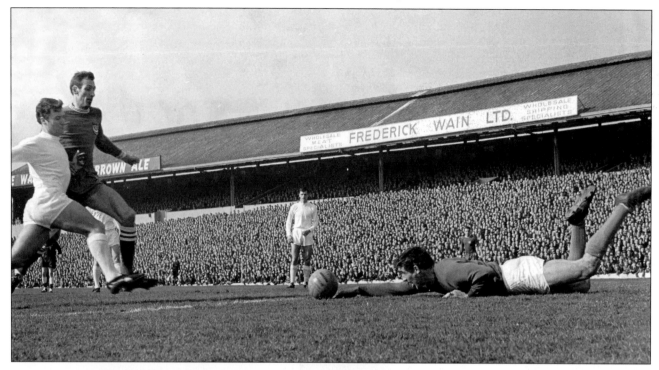

Albion were well in the FA Cup groove by the time they went to Portsmouth in round five in March, 1968, and withstood a spirited challenge from the Second Division side to go through 2-1. Here, John Osborne is at full stretch to keep Pompey at bay, with skipper Graham Williams playing his part, too. Eddie Colquhoun is the other player pictured for an Albion side who had earlier knocked out two other southern sides, Colchester and Southampton.

Reinforcements on the way for Albion's big FA Cup quarter-final replay date on Merseyside. Skipper Graham Williams (left) and Bobby Hope (standing in train doorway) prepare to depart from New Street Station for Liverpool after missing the 0-0 League draw at Burnley two days earlier through injury. The Hawthorns squad, held 0-0 at home by Bill Shankly's team, remained up north after playing at Turf Moor and were also strengthened by two travelling reserves, Rick Sheppard and (far right) Kenny Stephens.

Well-deserved moments of reflection in the visitors' dressing room for Alan Ashman as he ponders a job well done in Albion's FA Cup quarter-final replay at Anfield. His side held mighty Liverpool 1-1 thanks to a second-half headed equaliser by Jeff Astle in the shadow of The Kop after Tony Hateley had fired the favourites in front. Williams figured but Hope didn't in a performance that left the manager full of pride in his first season at the club.

Liverpool boss Bill Shankly does the talking as usual as replay arrangements are discussed after his side had drawn for the second time in nine days with Albion. Baggies secretary Alan Everiss joins his manager in making sure the venue for the third meeting is acceptable to both clubs. Old Trafford was originally chosen for the decider, only for Maine Road to then be selected when Manchester United decided their pitch was in danger of over-use.

First blood to Albion in their FA Cup quarter-final second replay against Liverpool at Manchester City as Jeff Astle holds off Ron Yeats (left) and Chris Lawler to drill an early left-foot shot inside Tommy Lawrence's near post. The strike took Astle's tally in the competition that season to seven but the Merseysiders produced a powerful response and levelled before half-time through a Tony Hateley header.

Bring on the Blues! Jeff Astle sees that some liquid refreshment is put to an alternative use as he gives fellow scorer Clive Clark a cooling-off in the Maine Road dressing room. The talented left-winger, who had also netted against Colchester and Portsmouth in rounds three and five respectively, rounded off a brilliant Albion move with the 67th minute winner that set up an all-Midlands semi-final against Birmingham at Villa Park.

ASHMAN: CUP WINNER

Bank Holidays were even busier for footballers four decades ago….this Easter Monday visit by Newcastle to The Hawthorns came three days after Albion drew 2-2 at St James's Park. And a home game against Sheffield Wednesday was thrown in for good measure in between. Albion drew 1-1 with Wednesday but beat visiting Newcastle 2-0 with both goals coming from Tony Brown, the man looking in on this piece of high kicking by Jeff Astle.

Albion's players are all smiles as they wade through the messages of congratulation after reaching the FA Cup final for the tenth time. This happy scene featuring (from left) Graham Williams, Jeff Astle, Tony Brown, John Osborne and John Talbut is from two days after the semi-final victory, and Hawthorns life was about to become even happier with a 6-3 home victory over title-chasing Manchester United on the same day.

Cup Final capers - a group of buoyant fans prepare to let the train take the strain as they set off for London and Albion's Wembley date with Everton. Harry Catterick's team were in highly impressive form and were warm favourites, having won 6-2 at The Hawthorns in the League a few weeks earlier, with Alan Ball scoring four. The forecasts were for a classic spectacle served up by two sides committed to attack.....

.....the reality was somewhat different, though. A turgid 90 minutes brought no goals and the occasional call from the crowd for football. Albion's solid white line holds firm here as John Osborne, supported by Doug Fraser (right) and forward-turned-defender John Kaye, catches a centre under pressure from Joe Royle. It wasn't Royle who broke the deadlock early in the 30 minutes of extra-time but the other no 9, Jeff Astle.

Match-winner Jeff Astle (left) basks in the glory and Wembley sunshine as realisation dawns. Albion are about to go and lift the FA Cup and manager Alan Ashman and his no 2 Stuart Williams extend their thanks and congratulations, starting with Dennis Clarke, who had gone on for the injured John Kaye and become the first substitute used in the final of the competition. In the background is dejected Everton forward Jimmy Husband, who missed a great chance of heading the winner in normal time.

This way to the Royal Box.....skipper Graham Williams and manager Ashman organise their troops ready for the climb up the famous 39 steps. Presenting the Cup on that historic day in May, 1968, was Princess Alexandra.

Skipper Graham Williams and match-winner Jeff Astle keep a safe grip on the treasured silverware as Albion players, with their partners, enjoy the post-match banquet in London's Park Lane Hotel. Also pictured are Dennis Clarke and Ian Collard, with keeper John Osborne partly visible at the rear. Below: Happiness is.......lapping it up as FA Cup winners. Dennis Clarke, watched by non-playing reserve Ray Fairfax, has the pleasant task of handing out some gifts to the ladyfolk. Fairfax, also a full-back, left for Northampton later that year.

Singing in the rain are the masses that packed West Bromwich High Street for the return of Albion's victorious players. Everyone, it seemed, wanted to be part of the joy of the club lifting the FA Cup for the fifth time.

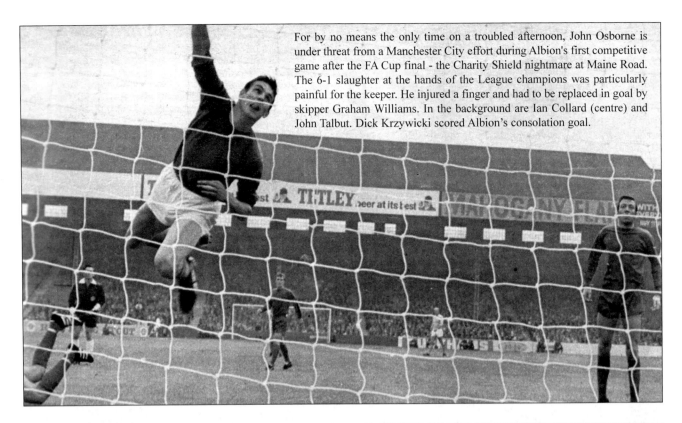

For by no means the only time on a troubled afternoon, John Osborne is under threat from a Manchester City effort during Albion's first competitive game after the FA Cup final - the Charity Shield nightmare at Maine Road. The 6-1 slaughter at the hands of the League champions was particularly painful for the keeper. He injured a finger and had to be replaced in goal by skipper Graham Williams. In the background are Ian Collard (centre) and John Talbut. Dick Krzywicki scored Albion's consolation goal.

Three cheers for the 'home internationals'! Doug Fraser (left), Bobby Hope and Ronnie Rees receive tankards from the club early in the 1968-69 season to commemorate call-ups from their countries. Fraser and Hope played twice apiece for Scotland while two of Rees' 39 Welsh caps were won while he was at The Hawthorns. Albion were to have a reasonable League season despite a shock League Cup KO at Peterborough at the second hurdle following an opening victory away to Nottingham Forest.

Albion In Europe

(Part One)

John Kaye challenges Utrecht keeper Hoogeveen on November 2, 1966, in Albion's first-ever European tie. The Inter Cities Fairs Cup trip to Holland pitched Jimmy Hagan's League Cup winners against a group of part-timers but a poor performance brought only a 1-1 draw despite the lead given them by Bobby Hope's first-half goal. Jeff Astle and no 11 Clive Clark are the players in support in a tie that drew a crowd of only 5,500 on a night so cold that, in the press box, the ink in one journalist's pen froze.

Centre-forward John Kaye is again the threat in the return against Utrecht on November 16, 1966. This effort, watched by Jeff Astle, didn't go in but Kaye did strike with a sweet left-foot shot for goal no 4 in Albion's 5-2 romp. The star of the evening, though, was Tony Brown, who marked his return from a two-month back injury by scoring a hat-trick, the first of them from the penalty spot.

Albion were half-way through their League Cup semi-final tie with West Ham when they flew to Italy to do battle with Bologna in the Fairs Cup third round on February 1, 1967. And they were no match for a side containing 1966 World Cup star Helmut Haller as they crashed to a 3-0 first-leg defeat in which the West German scored the third goal. Tony Brown finds himself heavily outnumbered in this attack on keeper Giuseppe Vavassori's goalmouth. Domestically, Albion were in considerable relegation danger at the time.

Five weeks separated the two legs of Albion's Fairs Cup clash with Bologna - and that made their death in the competition even slower. Tony Brown's header, watched by Jeff Astle, is shut out here on an evening on which Ray Fairfax provided a rare highlight in a 3-1 second-leg defeat with his only goal in 92 senior games for the club. Albion were beaten 6-1 on aggregate and Bologna had the misfortune to lose to Leeds in the next round on the drawing of lots after a 1-1 draw overall.

Flashpoints aplenty in FA Cup holders Albion's first-ever game in the European Cup Winners Cup - the first leg against Bruges in Belgium on September 18, 1968. Above: Clive Clark appears to be demanding a penalty from the Danish referee, who instead awards a free-kick just outside the penalty area as skipper Graham Williams arrives on the scene as peace-maker. Below: Doug Fraser and Clive Clark find themselves in a real melee in the Bruges penalty area. Jeff Astle's evening ended with him being carried off unconscious and taken to hospital following an incident that led to scores of spectators invading the pitch and some 20 police needing to restore order. Seventeen-year-old Asa Hartford equalised to become the youngest British goalscorer in any European competition but Albion were still facing an early exit after losing 3-1.

Justice done! Captain Graham Williams trots towards the back-slappers (right) after Albion overcame Bruges 2-0 to make European Cup Winners Cup progress on a stormy night at The Hawthorns. The left-back had to appeal to the crowd for calm at one point as the Belgians again adopted an over-physical approach but first-half strikes by Asa Hartford and Tony Brown saw his side through on the away goals rule. Above: One of the few occasions on which Jeff Astle was left on his feet! The striker, already with ten goals to his credit for the season, again had a battering from his markers all evening and was perhaps surprised to be left relatively unscathed in this first-half attack in which he is joined by (from left) Ronnie Rees, Clive Clark and John Talbut. Albion had gone out of the League Cup at Peterborough and lost 4-0 in the League away to their Wembley victors Everton in between the two legs against Bruges.

Striding out at Birmingham Airport are (from left) Dick Krzywicki, Doug Fraser, Tony Brown, Ray Wilson, Ian Collard, Dennis Martin, Asa Hartford, John Osborne and Evening Mail journalist Dennis Shaw. The group have their bags packed for a chilly mid-November trip to Rumania, where Albion were to play Dinamo Bucharest in the second round of the 1968-69 European Cup Winners Cup.

Not this time for Asa Hartford as he goes close with a shot away to Dinamo Bucharest. But he was on target in the first half of a 1-1 draw that brought him his third goal in three Euro ties and ended the side's run of three games without scoring. The Wednesday afternoon clash continued Albion's unfortunate knack of finding trouble against foreign opponents, though. Ronnie Rees was sent off for retaliation and missiles were thrown at the final whistle.

Characteristic Bomber..... trusty Tony Brown drills in a ferocious right-foot shot that leaves another keeper glad to get out of the way as the ball hurtles at speed to the net. This successful conversion, in the second half of the second leg with Dinamo on November 27, was Brown's second goal and Albion's third in a straightforward 4-0 win. Bobby Hope looks on. More than 33,000 attended both this return and the one versus Bruges at the earlier stage.

Jeff Astle retrieves the ball from the net during the rout of the Rumanians Dinamo Bucharest. Albion, again opting to change to their lucky all white strip, were barely extended despite the absence of the suspended Ronnie Rees and marched through by the thoroughly convincing margin of 5-1. As well as a brace from Tony Brown, Alan Ashman's side also had efforts from Astle and Graham Lovett to savour as they made sure of going one step further than in their Inter Cities Fairs Cup adventure of 1966-67.

ALBION IN EUROPE

The third phase of Albion's 1968-69 European Cup Winners Cup challenge took them north to Dunfermline, where a 0-0 first-leg draw left them well placed to justify their position as favourites to advance. Tony Brown goes close here to breaking the deadlock in chilly Scotland with an angled shot that just clears the bar during Albion's third clean sheet in four post-Christmas games. The odd one out was a 1-0 League defeat at Liverpool, where they lost to a late goal.

Where's that lucky white strip when you need it? Dennis Martin, deputising for Bobby Hope, just misses out in Albion's ECWC quarter-final KO against Dunfermline in February, 1969. After the 0-0 draw at East End Park, the Scots won the return by the only goal - scored in the second minute - and were beaten by eventual winners Slovan Bratislava in the semi-final. It was such a cold night at The Hawthorns that all Albion's players except Graham Lovett wore gloves.

Still A Major Force

No 7 Ronnie Rees, signed from Coventry the previous spring, prepares to run into the arms of Ian Collard as he savours opening the scoring in the 6-1 Hawthorns thrashing of his former club on October 9, 1968. It was the second in a run of four successive League wins for Albion. Rees, a Welsh international winger, netted 12 goals in 41 games for the club before being joining Nottingham Forest.

Still happy to show off the FA Cup early in 1968-69.....happy in the company of their hosts are (from left) coach Stuart Williams, Jeff Astle, Ronnie Rees, manager Alan Ashman, Clive Clark, John Talbut and Graham Williams.

Albion's players hare off in joyous celebration of a spectacular late Tony Brown winner in the Hawthorns clash with Arsenal on October 19, 1968. Only three minutes remained when the goal-grabber supreme scored with a ferocious free-kick from well outside the area to bring his side maximum points at home to the Gunners for the first time since 1963. A leaping Asa Hartford, no 12 Graham Williams and Lyndon Hughes join Brown in enjoying the moment to the full. The sides were to meet again at Highbury two months later.....

Arsenal striker Bobby Gould, later to serve both as a player and as a manager at The Hawthorns, tangles with John Osborne and left-back Ray Wilson in a Highbury mudbath on December 21, 1968. The Gunners duly took their revenge as an own goal by new skipper Doug Fraser and a more conventional effort from Gould condemned Albion to a 2-0 defeat. Ashman's men were back in London a week later and thrashed QPR 4-0.

Brief hope for travel-weary Albion at home to Southampton on January 18, 1969. Tony Brown beats Gerry Gurr to halve a two-goal deficit but the Saints hung on to record a League double over a side against whom they had also recorded a win and a draw in the previous season's First Division programme. Maybe tiredness was the reason for Albion's erratic performance - they had drawn at Dunfermline in the midweek in the European Cup Winners Cup.

A joyous Jeff Astle salutes the Tony Brown cracker that kept Albion on the FA Cup trail in their fifth-round home tie against Arsenal on February 12, 1969. More than 45,000 braved an icy night to witness a game postponed because of snow four days earlier - and Bomber's 67th minute special sent most of them home happy. Albion played only one League match that month because of the freeze and had fixtures at Sunderland and at home to Ipswich called off.

All Scots together....(from left) Ray Wilson, Asa Hartford, Doug Fraser and Bobby Hope put up with some familiar north-of-the-border weather amid Albion's bid for more success in the knockout competitions. In an unwelcome twist to the tartan theme, the club had just gone out of the European Cup Winners Cup to Dunfermline but were still going strong in the FA Cup, starting their defence with wins over Second Division duo Norwich at The Hawthorns and Fulham at Craven Cottage.

A familiar late 1960s sight as Albion's players train on the sands of Southport. The Lancashire resort was a frequent destination for Alan Ashman's squad during their halcyon cup-fighting days and was used on this occasion before the FA Cup quarter-final trip to Chelsea in March, 1969. Tony Brown, Bobby Hope and Jeff Astle are the trio being put through their paces, with Clive Clark and John Osborne next in line. The all white gear, as match-day kit or in the tracksuit line, was another well-known feature at the time.

The Southport getaway obviously worked once more because Albion emerged from Stamford Bridge with one of their best-ever FA Cup scalps, although it needed this well-struck left-foot Tony Brown equaliser to steady the ship following a headed early goal by Dave Webb at the other end. Alan Ashman's side were growing to like playing in London in the capital, having won at Wembley a few months earlier and at Fulham at the second stage of their defence. Jeff Astle and Dennis Martin look on here.

Another dramatic image from the chastening of Chelsea….. a moment of major controversy as Jeff Astle's second-half header arrows towards the net, only for the referee to cut short Albion's goal celebrations by awarding a penalty instead. Tony Brown saw his spot-kick brilliantly saved by Peter Bonetti but Astle tucked away the winner shortly afterwards in the 59th minute.

A prone John Osborne awaits the physio's arrival after he had taken a buffeting while somehow sitting on a last-minute Chelsea effort and sparking a heated melee. The 2-1 victory at Stamford Bridge represented a third successive London scalp in the competition for the holders, who were becoming increasingly confident of winning the Cup for the second season running.

The day Albion's grip on the FA Cup was broken. Hillsborough did not prove a happy hunting ground in the late 1960s and early 1970s and was the stage for this surprise defeat against relegation-bound Leicester on March 29, 1969. Ashman's men played poorly and lost to an 87th minute goal by Willenhall-born former Baggies fan Allan Clarke. Here, no 11 Asa Hartford watches John Kaye clear while Jeff Astle tumbles and Doug Fraser and Ray Wilson cover the line.

Albion's Hillsborough hopes are briefly raised by a header by John Kaye, who pops up to try his luck from in between Andy Lochhead (left) and Alan Woollett. Waiting to pick up the pieces are Tony Brown and a half-hidden Dennis Martin. The defeat, watched by over 53,000, was the side's first in 15 ties in the competition stretching back well over two years to a 5-0 fourth-round thrashing at Leeds.

With two promising cup runs having petered out in the latter stages, Albion were left with only a high League placing to chase in what remained of 1968-69. And, helped by this early Dick Krzywicki goal in a 1-1 home draw against a Leeds side shortly to be crowned League champions for the first time, they ended the season strongly. Albion were unbeaten in their final eight games and finished tenth.

Youth Cup Heroics

Cheers lads! Coach Jimmy Dunn pours a celebratory drink after Albion beat Chelsea to reach the final of the 1968-69 FA Youth Cup. Pictured (standing, from left): Len Cantello, Gordon Nisbet, Alistair Robertson, Sid Bell, Jim Holton, Lyndon Hughes, Roger Minton. Seated: Asa Hartford, Keith Morton and Hugh MacLean. Five of the players made 100 or more first-team appearances for Albion while the late Holton, a powerful centre-half, departed as a youngster but enjoyed a fine career with both Manchester United and Scotland.

Stewart Woolgar goes round keeper Swinburne to make it 2-0 in Albion's home first leg of the FA Youth Cup final against Sunderland at the end of April, 1969. The Chesterfield-born midfielder, who would play only six senior games for the club before switching to Doncaster, scored twice in this first leg of the final in front of a crowd of nearly 17,000 but it all went wrong in a nightmare second leg on Wearside a week later.

Albion's 3-0 first-leg victory counted for little when they arrived at Roker Park for the second leg of the 1968-69 FA Youth Cup final. The sendings-off of Scottish duo Asa Hartford and Jim Holton did nothing for their chances and they caved in to a nightmare 6-0 defeat that left Sunderland celebrating. Coach Jimmy Dunn is pictured among (from left) Len Cantello, Sid Bell, Keith Morton, Lyndon Hughes, keeper Gordon Nisbet, no 6 Alistair Robertson and Hugh MacLean, with an obvious picking-up job on his hands.

Albion DID get their hands on the FA Youth Cup in 1976, just a few days after the club had won promotion back to the top flight. The youngsters set themselves up with a 2-0 victory at Wolves in the first leg of the final and completed the job by winning the return 3-1. Director Cliff Edwards is the director in charge of champagne here as coach Albert McPherson, alongside striker Derek Monaghan at the front, keeps a hand on the silverware. Also pictured are (from left) Mark Grew, Mark Trenter, Brian Clarke, Derek Statham, Wayne Hughes, Derek Hood, Tony Cooper, Colin Gregson, John Loveridge, Kevin Summerfield and Martin Davies.

Albion had three new players on board for the start of the 1969-70 campaign as they attempted to turn cup heroics into genuine League success. In an unfamiliar spending spree, manager Alan Ashman was allowed to recruit club record signing Colin Suggett for £100,000 from Sunderland, Danny Hegan (fourth from the right) from Ipswich and Allan Glover from QPR. Youngsters like Hughie Reed and Alan Merrick (both just to Ashman's right) were also emerging among senior survivors like Williams, Osborne, Fraser, Talbut and Kaye.

Opening-day joy very quickly wore off for Albion in 1969-70. Having won their first fixture, against Southampton away, with two Colin Suggett goals, they promptly suffered a 3-1 follow-up defeat at Coventry. Here, John Talbut is beaten by the punch of Sky Blues keeper Bill Glazier on an evening when the opposite no 1, pictured in the distance, is Gordon Nisbet.

FOREVER ALBION

Percy Freeman, a former lorry driver and nightclub bouncer who was recruited to The Hawthorns from Stourbridge, discomforts Arsenal keeper Bob Wilson on August 16, 1969. Ian Ure takes evasive action on an afternoon when Albion were being beaten for the second successive game. They also soon lost their return clash with Coventry and suffered five defeats in their opening seven League matches.

Despite their League failings, Albion made a winning start in the 1969-70 League Cup when they made the short trip to Second Division Villa in early September and ran out 2-1 winners. Colin Suggett and Jeff Astle scored their goals either side of this effort at the other end from Barrie Hole which just creeps in at John Osborne's near post, watched by (from left) John Talbut, Astle, John Kaye and Doug Fraser.

More League Cup success as Bobby Hope flashes a shot at goal in the fifth-round replay at home to Leicester on Bonfire Night, 1969. Peter Shilton could only block and, from the rebound, Jeff Astle scored the second of his two goals in a 2-1 win that put Albion through to their fifth semi-final in five years in the major cup competitions. The sides had drawn 0-0 at Filbert Street a week earlier, Albion having prevailed at The Hawthorns against Ipswich and Bradford City in the previous two rounds, Ipswich's KO coming in a replay.

Astle, left foot, Everton the opponents….. a highly familiar plot! The Merseysiders were again on the receiving end as The King struck the first of Albion's two goals in a 2-0 home League win on November 8, 1969. Dick Krzywicki netted the other. Brian Labone and Alan Ball are the players in view for Everton, who were to win the League that season, clinching it with a victory by the same score over Albion at Goodison Park on April Fool's Day.

Second Division Carlisle proved a tough nut to crack in the League Cup semi-final and actually led after the first leg with a late goal set up by George McVitie - a winger later to join Albion. John Kaye is denied (above) with an effort at Brunton Park, where the Cumbrians had three efforts cleared off the line as well as hitting the woodwork once. It wasn't plain sailing in the return a fortnight later, either, with Alan Ashman's former side holding out for 54 minutes, during which John Talbut had to go off injured. But Bobby Hope finally broke through and Colin Suggett, Tony Brown and substitute Dennis Martin added the others that secured a 4-2 aggregate success and left the home dressing room a happy place (below) as the sidelined Graham Williams shared out the bubbly.

STILL A MAJOR FORCE

Graham Williams came to the end of the road in this 2-0 League defeat at Derby on December 27, 1969. It was the 26-cap Welshman's 360th and last appearance in a club career that was spent entirely at The Hawthorns, where Albion had beaten West Ham 3-1 the day before. Williams was to become involved on the coaching side at the club but was unable to contain the threat of John O'Hare in his final outing, the forward scoring both of the goals at the Baseball Ground.

The goal Tony Brown rated as the best of the club record 279 he scored in League and cups for Albion......the ball speeds towards the bottom corner of the net after a stunning first-time half-volley from 25 yards. The moment was captured by Match of the Day and a eulogising Barry Davies but Sheffield Wednesday scored twice at the other end, also in the second half, to condemn Albion to an FA Cup third-round exit at Hillsborough - the ground where they had lost in the semi-final the previous year.

A Wembley Return

Albion's players find an innovative way of discussing League Cup final tactics in the grounds of the Selsdon Park Hotel in London. Graham Williams (crouching, left) is the one talking things through in a picture-postcard setting a couple of days before the clash with a Manchester City side who had won the FA Cup the previous year and the League Championship the year before that.

Alas, the combination of the wintry weather and the staging of the Horse of the Year Show shortly before meant Wembley was not as attractive as Albion's hotel grounds. In mudbath conditions, the 1966 League Cup winners were off to a flier with a fifth minute Jeff Astle header, the striker also causing City problems here as he sets off in possession with Colin Suggett at his side.

A WEMBLEY RETURN

Jeff Astle is again the threat to the Manchester City goal as he goes in at full stretch on keeper Joe Corrigan (left).

City hit back hard and, although Albion still led near the hour, Mike Doyle equalised, then Glyn Pardoe struck the winner in extra-time. Ashman's men had their moments but Corrigan, recently a goalkeeper coach at The Hawthorns, denied John Talbut and Colin Suggett (below). City lifted the European Cup Winners Cup as well a few weeks later.

Levelling Out

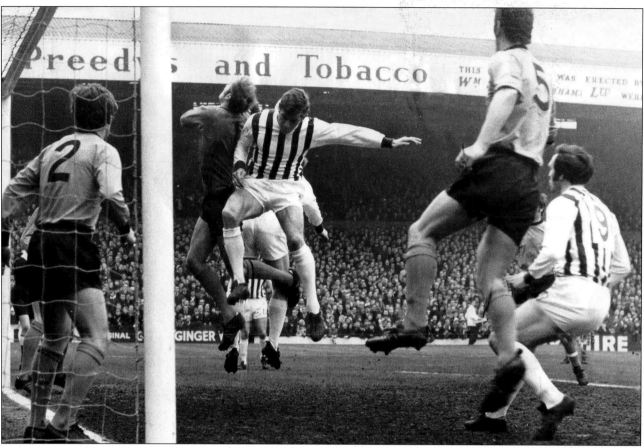

John Kaye is beaten by the safe handling of Wolves keeper John Oldfield in the centenary clash of the Black Country rivals on February 28, 1970. The 100th meeting of the clubs, a week before Albion took on Manchester City in the League Cup final, ended in a 3-3 draw, with Jeff Astle (right) and Colin Suggett (2) on target. Bernard Shaw and Dave Woodfield are the covering Wolves defenders.

Jeff Astle ended 1969-70 with 30 Albion goals - including one in this home draw with Spurs in late March. Cyril Knowles (left) and John Collins struggle to cope as the no 9 demonstrates the form that would earn him a place in the England World Cup squad to Mexico. Albion beat Chelsea two days later, then hammered Nottingham Forest but finished a disappointing 16th - their lowest placing for 15 years.

Cup action of a different kind as John Talbut (right) and Lyndon Hughes challenge against Lanerossi Vicenza in the first game in the Anglo Italian Cup in May, 1970. The tie finished 0-0 but the return in Italy a fortnight later was abandoned as a 1-1 draw because of fighting. In their other two matches, Albion beat Roma 4-0 at home and drew 1-1 with them away.

Jeff Astle makes his presence felt in this aerial challenge in a pre-season clash at Villa Park in 1970 against a side just relegated to the Third Division. A Mick Wright own goal brought Albion a 1-1 draw in front of almost 21,000 fans, Graham Lovett appearing in the background of this picture.

Is that meant to be me? John Osborne studies a doll for personal likeness after a fan sent Albion players lucky mascots at the start of 1970-71. Scots Ray Wilson and Hughie Reed are seen either side of Jeff Astle, who was recently back from the World Cup in Mexico. The centre-forward won two of his five senior caps as England reached the quarter-finals before losing in extra-time to West Germany.

Hughie Reed shoots just wide in Albion's 3-1 League Cup second-round win at home to Second Division Charlton on September 8, 1970. John Kaye, Jeff Astle and Colin Suggett scored the goals but the night was soured when Alistair Robertson suffered a badly broken leg that would keep him out for more than 12 months. Albion won at Preston in the next round, only for their League Cup run to then dissolve with a 5-0 thrashing at Tottenham.

Tony Brown bludgeons home Albion's winner against Brian Clough's Derby at The Hawthorns on September 26, 1970. George McVitie, signed from Carlisle shortly before, netted the first in what was a much-needed response from Alan Ashman's side to the shock of losing 6-2 to Arsenal at Highbury the previous Saturday. Derby gave a debut to Archie Gemmill and have Alan Durban, John Richardson and Willie Carlin tracking back in this incident from their 2-1 defeat.

A tap-in goal for George McVitie - his third in ten matches for the club - in Albion's 3-0 home win over League champions Everton on October 31, 1970. Tony Brown, already starting the celebrations, was the maker with a shot saved by keeper Andy Rankin and was also on the score-sheet along with Jeff Astle. It was the second of eight successive home wins Albion would record against the Merseysiders between 1969 and 1979.

Jeff Astle gets in between Coventry duo Geoff Strong (left) and Jeff Blockley in the 1-1 Boxing Day draw at a frozen Highfield Road in 1970. Depressingly, Albion had already gone more than a year without winning an away game and had John Wile making his second appearance for them here following a £32,000 move from Peterborough that proved superb business for his new club. It wasn't a great day for open play, both goals coming via penalties - from Neil Martin and Tony Brown.

FOREVER ALBION

Ray Wilson covers while Jim Cumbes takes control in Albion's FA Cup round-four letdown against Ipswich on January 23, 1971. Colin Suggett's goal seemed enough to secure victory until a scrambled last-gasp equaliser from the East Anglians, who then won 3-0 in a replay that proved to be Alan Ashman's last cup game in charge. Playing for Ipswich against Albion, who had needed two bites to beat Scunthorpe in round three, was Ian Collard (pictured background left).

Albion had suffered three straight League defeats when they beat bottom-of-the-table Burnley 1-0 at home on February 6, 1971. The decider came from Tony Brown - his 99th top-flight goal in his 300th appearance in all competitions - although Jeff Astle leads the charge here by harassing defender Colin Waldron. Brown had been with England to Malta in the midweek and would soon complete his League century in a 2-2 draw at Tottenham.

LEVELLING OUT

No joy for Jeff Astle and Albion in this home League meeting with Wolves on March 20, 1971. With Alan Ashman's side heavily dependent on their form at The Hawthorns, goals by George McVitie and Tony Brown failed to prevent the visitors striding to a 4-2 victory. Brown, a League ever-present, was on his way to a magnificent final haul of 30 goals for the season in all club competitions while Astle, pictured here holding off Wolves' John McAlle, managed 16.

George Best leaves Alan Merrick trailing and tries to outfox keeper Jim Cumbes as well on Manchester United's top-flight visit to The Hawthorns on March 6, 1971. As usual, when Matt Busby's side were in town, it was a goal-filled thriller, won by Albion, with boyhood United fan Tony Brown hitting a dream hat-trick before John Wile made it 4-3 with a last-gasp header.

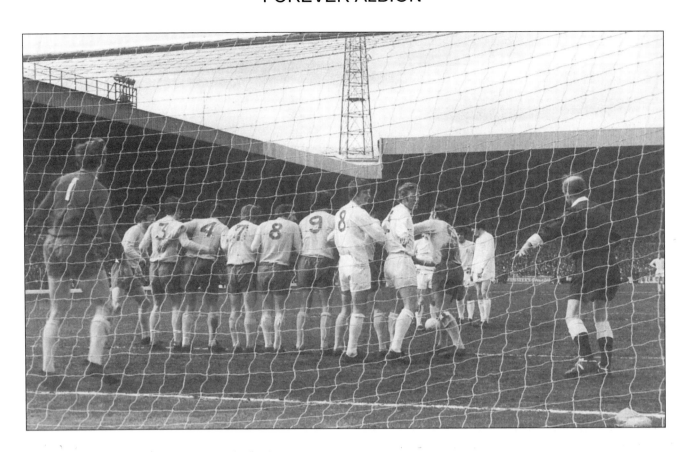

Barricades of different kinds on an extraordinary afternoon at Elland Road on April 17, 1971 ....above: John Kaye (far right) organises Albion's defensive wall to successfully withstand a Leeds free-kick from well inside the penalty area. From left are Jim Cumbes, John Wile, Alan Merrick, Graham Lovett, Colin Suggett, Tony Brown, Jeff Astle, Lyndon Hughes and Kaye. Bobby Hope and Asa Hartford were covering the posts. Albion were deservedly leading through a Brown shot on the run when the mood turned ugly with the decision to allow Astle's tap-in goal around the hour mark after Suggett had run back from an offside position. Rioting fans held the game up for several minutes before the blue line restored order and Leeds pulled one back near the end. Albion played brilliantly to hold on for their first win in eight games and their first away in the League for over 16 months. Leeds were ultimately pipped to the title by Arsenal.

Albion 1 Inter Milan 1 - not a bad scoreline to send Hawthorns regulars into the summer break! John Wile rises superbly to crash home a header in the opening game of the Anglo Italian Cup on May 26, 1971. It was a second venture into the tournament for Albion, who lost the return in Milan 1-0 in front of a modest 15,000 crowd.

Albion press through no 8 Tony Brown, watched by John Wile (left) and Bobby Hope, in the second of their Anglo Italian Cup games in the summer of 1971. This clash at home to Cagliari ended in an odd-goal defeat in front of more than 17,000 and, with a 1-0 defeat at the hands of the Italians in Sardinia six days later, Albion exited the tournament at the group stage. More seriously, they had won only one of their last 11 League games in finishing 17th and manager Alan Ashman paid with his job a few weeks later.

The Mauling of Man Utd
(Part One)

It was a result and evening that had the masses drooling - Albion 6 Manchester United 3 on April 29, 1968. It would have been a magnificent achievement at any time but this was all the more remarkable given that Alan Ashman's team had fought out and won a demanding FA Cup semi-final against Birmingham only two days before, and United were two points clear at the top at the time in their pursuit of a second consecutive League Championship. The official attendance was 45,992 but another 5,000 are said to have forced a way in without paying and 5,000 more were locked out. Those who got in witnessed one of The Hawthorns' most memorable nights as Matt Busby's United conceded six for the first time since a hammering at Burnley in 1963 and lost to Albion for the first time, home or away, in five and a half years. Five goal pictures from the game form the start of this special section, which definitely isn't for the eyes of United supporters!

Jeff Astle, who had struck early with his left foot in the FA Cup semi-final at Villa Park just over 48 hours earlier, did the same against United. This shot was drilled past Pat Crerand and keeper Alex Stepney from a narrow angle.

Goal no 2 followed in the 39th minute from Ronnie Rees, a winger who was Cup-tied after moving from Coventry only a few weeks before. Ian Collard is up in support but is not needed as an unerring left-foot shot proves more than good enough to find the target.

Albion knew it was their night when Tony Brown made it 3-0 from a penalty in the 59th minute, his first kick having been saved, only for the referee to order a retake because Alex Stepney moved too early.

Jeff Astle having made it 4-0, Asa Hartford turns away in delight here after tucking in his first goal in League football - in only his second start in the First Division. Graham Lovett salutes the big moment in the fledgling career of the teenage Scottish midfielder. A Denis Law penalty had previously cut United's arrears to three.

And Astle dives to steer home the header that brought him his sixth hat-trick for the club and Albion their sixth and final goal. It also meant The King had overtaken Jimmy Greaves as the country's leading scorer on 31. United pulled two back late on through Brian Kidd but had handed the initiative to Manchester City in the title race and it was their neighbours who would be crowned champions a few weeks later. Remarkably, Astle scored another hat-trick, against West Ham, only two nights after these individual and team heroics.

Fast forward to 1968-69 and John Talbut causes danger to Manchester United's goal as he challenges for a high ball with Nobby Stiles. Ian Collard looks on during an evening on which Albion, playing their second game of the season after a goalless home draw with Sheffield Wednesday, won 3-1 with goals by Jeff Astle (2) and Tony Brown. The victory meant Albion had scored nine goals against United in two meetings at The Hawthorns either side of their FA Cup final triumph.

A rare penalty miss by Tony Brown as he sees his shot saved by Alex Stepney in the League clash at The Hawthorns on October 25, 1969. Bobby Hope and Asa Hartford are the Albion players on the edge of the area, with John Aston the United man with hands on hips. Bomber didn't get another chance from the spot that season as this was the Baggies' only penalty of 1969-70 but he scored later in this game in open play and Hope hit the decider in another exciting victory, this time by the closer margin of 2-1.

Another shot of the 1969-70 clash as John Talbut lends his weight to an Albion attack and leaves United forward Brian Kidd grounded.

Another Albion v United epic, settled by this last-minute John Wile header, on March 6, 1971. The centre-half's second goal in successive games saw Albion home 4-3 after he scored in a 3-3 draw at Everton the previous Saturday. Tony Brown had earlier scored a hat-trick in a roller-coaster of a game against United that proved to be the side's final home victory under Alan Ashman. They won only one of their remaining 11 matches - famously at Leeds - and the manager was sacked in the summer.

Two of United's all-time superstars threaten their markers at The Hawthorns on January 29, 1972. But, in front of a 46,992 crowd, Denis Law (left) and George Best had to admit second best, although their side were top of the table before kick-off. Albion fell behind to a Best penalty but Bobby Gould equalised and Jeff Astle headed the decider in a 2-1 win. John Osborne is the keeper here, with John Wile and no 2 Gordon Nisbet also helping to keep things tight.

Storm Clouds Gather

New season, new boss…..former Hawthorns hero Don Howe took over in July, 1971, and set about making Albion a tougher nut to crack. The accent was more on physical fitness as (from left) Alan Merrick, Jim Cumbes, Hugh MacLean, Len Cantello, Alistair Robertson, John Osborne, Lyndon Hughes, Asa Hartford and Colin Suggett found out. John Talbut had by now gone and others would soon follow.

A day-one meeting for Don Howe with the two main Hawthorns scorers he inherited, Jeff Astle and Tony Brown. Alas, injury problems became an increasing feature of Astle's professional life while Brown was asked by the new boss to play in a role that didn't suit him; so much so that the club's record marksman thought long and hard about a transfer.

Don Howe's priorities included making Albion harder to beat, more physical and, as demonstrated here by midfielder Len Cantello under the gaze of Bobby Hope and Ray Wilson, fitter. From the opening pre-season friendlies, the side revealed a more robust nature aimed at stemming the alarming flow of goals against that had until recently contributed to them going more than 16 months without an away win.

Boby Hope clips his kick past Colchester keeper Graham Smith in a shoot-out in the final of the Watney Cup pre-season competition at The Hawthorns in 1971. Albion lost to the Fourth Division club on penalties after a 4-4 draw, having won at Wrexham and Halifax in the earlier stages. Smith made enough of an impression to be signed by Albion a few weeks later, although his stay was brief.

Albion won their first two League games under Don Howe - at West Ham and at home to Everton - and topped the table as a result. But the optimism didn't last and, following a home draw with Coventry, they lost for the first time when a George Best-inspired Manchester United beat them 3-1 despite this threat to Alex Stepney's goal from John Wile. The game, played at Stoke because of crowd trouble at Old Trafford the previous season, saw Tony Brown score for the fourth successive match under Howe.

The rot had set in by the time Ipswich won 2-1 at The Hawthorns on September 18, 1971. It was Albion's fourth straight League defeat and they hadn't won in seven Division One games while also going out of the League Cup at home to Tottenham. Tony Brown, on target against the East Anglians, scored all but one of his side's goals in the first 12 matches. Here, Ray Wilson boots clear watched by John Kaye - making his last but one home appearance before joining Hull - and Jim Cumbes.

The Asa Hartford Affair

Asa Hartford's world was turned upside down in a few days in November, 1971. The Scottish midfielder joined Leeds for £170,000 from Albion and was pictured training with them (above). But a medical revealed an extremely rare hole-in-the-heart condition - and a series of meetings and consultations left he and Hawthorns boss Don Howe resigned to the deal being called off (right).

It was a story that rocked football, with Hartford facing a decidedly uncertain future at the tender age of 21, and he was subsequently quizzed by Midlands journalists in the company of his manager and Albion physio George Wright (background right).

THE ASA HARTFORD AFFAIR

Thankfully, it wasn't long before Hartford was back doing what he enjoyed most and he returned to the training ground with Albion in a few days. Here, he takes a breather while coach Brian Whitehouse and midfielder Allan Glover get things organised.

The 21-year-old was all smiles when he was welcomed back to the fold for the short trip to Nottingham Forest and had the Canadian Glen Johnson for company when boarding the bus. Hartford was ultimately to join Manchester City for £225,000 three years later and continued to play with a boundless energy that brought him well in excess of 900 appearances, 50 of them for Scotland. He played 275 times for Albion and proceeded to serve countless other clubs.

Eddie Colquhoun, by now in Sheffield United's colours, produces a decisive clearing header to put paid to an Albion attack led by Bobby Gould (left) and John Wile in the 2-2 home League draw on January 8, 1972. Tony Brown netted twice for a side who had bounced back from a grim pre-Christmas sequence of seven consecutive defeats by beating Liverpool at home and Ipswich at Portman Road in successive games. Brown had scored 13 of the 21 goals his struggling side managed in all competitions in 1971-72 up to the middle of January.

John Wile threatens Coventry's goal in Albion's 2-1 FA Cup third-round KO at The Hawthorns in January, 1972. Bobby Gould, signed from Wolves a few months earlier and facing another of his old clubs here, is the player wearing no 9 while Len Cantello is on the right. Chris Chilton is Coventry's centre-forward and the no 6 is Bobby Parker, who astonishingly got away unpunished when punching away a shot close to the line to deny Tony Brown another goal.

STORM CLOUDS GATHER

Albion, in serious relegation peril in mid-season, had as good as guaranteed safety by the time of this 1-0 home defeat against Leeds on April 22, 1972. By winning eight and drawing five of the previous 16 League matches, they had virtually booked a 24th successive year in the top-flight, so weren't particularly concerned at losing to a Johnny Giles penalty. No 9 Tony Brown watches Asa Hartford threaten a team who won the 1972 FA Cup and also went within a fraction of the title.

Tony Brown almost moved on during Don Howe's reign but remained easily the club's leading scorer. After hitting the 20 mark once more in 1971-72, he had to wait until this winner at home to League champions Derby on September 9 to break his Division One duck the season after, the manager having signed Ally Brown (no 10) from Leicester the previous spring. Albion, who also had Bobby Gould on target, were already back in trouble after another poor start.

The Browns are again in harness here but it was Colin Suggett who scored the only goal of the First Division derby at home to Coventry on September 23, 1972. Albion's third successive League victory was watched by only 15,373, though, and the football remained less than exhilarating. Bill Glazer is the Sky Blues keeper and Roy Barry the defender to the left. In Albion's goal, with John Osborne out of favour, is youngster Peter Latchford.

Albion, having beaten QPR at the first hurdle, reached the end of the League Cup trail when confronted by Liverpool at the next stage. Not that they didn't give Bill Shankly's men a fright - in fact, they took them to a replay and then lost by the odd goal at Anfield on an evening when Ally Robertson scored only his second first-team goal. Here at The Hawthorns, Bobby Gould worries Larry Lloyd, no 4 Tommy Smith and Peter Cormack but Asa Hartford was the marksman in a 1-1 draw.

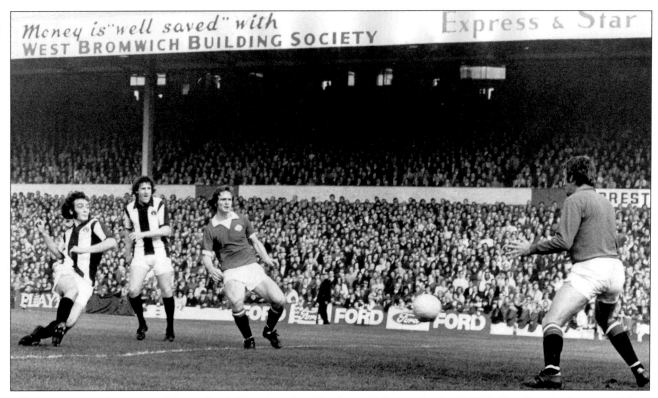

Ally Brown sweeps home one of his two first-half goals against Manchester United on October 7, 1972. Tony Brown, also pictured, later missed a penalty that would have made it 3-1 - and that was all the encouragement United needed to hit back for a 2-2 draw in George Best's last competitive appearance at The Hawthorns. In front of 39,209 crowd, the mercurial winger scored from a penalty to peg back the club against whom he had made his debut around a decade earlier.

Alistair Robertson, destined to play for Wolves a decade and a half later, hacks clear in Albion's 1-0 Black Country derby win at The Hawthorns on October 21, 1972. Bobby Gould scored the only goal against his former club, much to the disappointment of Derek Dougan, on whom Peter Latchford and John Wile keep an eye here. It was Albion's first victory in five games and they followed up by beating Newcastle in the first leg of their Texaco Cup second-round meeting, only to then go out in the return at St James' Park.

Don Howe rallies his players for extra-time in their FA Cup third-round marathon with Nottingham Forest in January, 1973. After a 1-1 draw at The Hawthorns, the City Ground replay was going the same way until abandoned because of fog late on. Then came this goalless third try to find a winner at Forest before Albion finally won 3-1 at Leicester with goals by Len Cantello, Asa Hartford and Colin Suggett.

Don Howe's four years as Albion boss won't go down as the highlight of his long career but he was at least responsible for attracting Willie Johnston to The Hawthorns. The dazzling, crowd-pleasing left-winger closes in here as Bob Wilson seizes possession in front of young Arsenal full-back Brendon Batson. This 1-0 Albion win on February 28, 1973, secured by Tony Brown's goal, came on the night Jeff Astle returned from chronic knee trouble to revive the club's fading hopes of avoiding the drop.

'Well saved' says the West Bromwich Building Society advert high on the stand roof. It's a different story for Chelsea keeper John Phillips, though, as Tony Brown helps himself to yet another goal. But this 1-1 home draw on March 10, 1973 was hardly enough for an Albion side sinking fast. They had lost at rivals-in-distress Manchester United the previous week and 2-0 defeats at Ipswich and Wolves shortly afterwards kept Hawthorns backs to the wall. Also pictured are (from left) Jeff Astle, John Wile, Alan Merrick and Peter Osgood.

Jeff Astle did his bit to try to stop Albion crashing through the trapdoor in the spring of 1973. Sidelined by injury until the end of February, the striker scored five times in the last 14 games for a side short on goals. His haul included efforts in the final two matches at home to Manchester City and at Birmingham, and also this one - the only goal of the game - at home to Leicester on April 7. David Shaw and no 11 Willie Johnston are about to weigh in with their congratulations. Tony Brown missed a penalty later in the afternoon.

The game that really did for Albion - a 1-0 home defeat against fellow strugglers Norwich on April 21, 1973. Having just beaten Leicester and Everton at The Hawthorns, hopes were high of another escape but this loss - secured by a David Cross goal near the end - was the final decisive turning point. Albion, represented here by Tony Brown and a distant Asa Hartford, ended the season with four defeats, finished rock bottom and were relegated with Crystal Palace. Cross later had two spells with the Baggies.

Welcome to the Second Division. If Albion thought their goal-scoring problems would disappear with lower-grade football, they were sadly mistaken. They averaged only one per game in the first third of the new season, with this 0-0 home draw with Bolton in front of 16,148 summing up their stuttering progress. Roy Greaves is the visiting player trying a shot while John Wile makes life as difficult as he can for him and Asa Hartford looks on. Photo courtesy of Bolton Evening News.

For eight days in January, 1974, Tony Brown was the scourge of Nottingham. In two games on successive Saturdays, he scored no fewer than seven goals, three in a 4-0 FA Cup third-round win at home to Second Division rivals County and then all four in a follow-up 4-1 League trouncing of Forest at the City Ground. One paper called it the most spectacular plundering in the East Midlands since the days of Robin Hood. County are thankful to survive this near miss in the Cup tie (above), with John Wile looking to pick up any pieces, while David Shaw is the nearest team-mate in attendance (below) and Willie Johnston is in the distance as Bomber puts away the first of his quartet at Forest. These were the last two of Brown's nine Baggies hat-tricks, the one against County making him the first Albion player to achieve the 'full set' of trebles in the League, FA Cup, League Cup and Europe. Bottom photo courtesy of Nottingham Evening Post.

Asa Hartford lunges for a high ball during Albion's first-ever Sunday fixture - the FA Cup fourth-round clash at Everton in front of 53,509 on January 27, 1974. The 0-0 draw was the first meeting of the clubs in the competition since the Baggies' Wembley win in 1968 and was shaded by the Second Division underdogs, who then won the replay 1-0 with a Tony Brown header. Also pictured here are fellow midfielder Len Cantello and Everton's David Clements.

Peter Latchford makes a brilliant save when all seems lost to help Albion retain their grip on the Second Division derby at Villa Park on March 2, 1974. Ray Graydon is the frustrated forward, with John Wile grounded and probably despairing on the right. Tony Brown (2) and Wile scored first-half goals to give Albion a 3-1 victory and their first double over Villa in nine years, a bumper 43,119 having seen the 2-0 Boxing Day home win at The Hawthorns. Don Howe's side went to Villa in good heart, having won at Carlisle five days earlier.

STORM CLOUDS GATHER

Having fallen away to finish in a miserable eighth spot in the spring of 1974, Albion made another mixed start as they set about doing better next time round. Two defeats and two wins preceded this 1-1 draw with Manchester United, no 10 Alan Merrick scoring the goal. John Wile launches himself at Alex Stepney here but couldn't stop Stuart Pearson netting for a just-relegated United side who went straight back up. No 12 Brian Greenhoff (right) had gone on as sub for Mick Martin, who was soon to join Albion. The players are wearing black armbands following the death the day before of the long-serving former Albion chairman Major Wilson Keys.

Below: One of two 1-1 Hawthorns draws in the autumn of 1974 between Albion and a Norwich side managed by John Bond. Alan Merrick was enjoying a mini purple patch as a goalscorer at the time but found his sights somewhat obscured in this raid towards the Birmingham Road End. David Shaw was on target but it was Albion's fourth successive League game without a win and the run was to stretch to six before they embarked on a trot of four straight victories. The sequences typified their up-and-down fortunes.

Albion were marooned in mid-table when they broke away from their League toils to again face Norwich, this time in round three of the League Cup on October 9, 1974. Dave Stringer scored an own goal to do what Tony Brown and Alistair Robertson couldn't do here - beat keeper Kevin Keelan - but Albion had to settle for another 1-1 draw. Norwich won 2-0 in the replay after extra-time.

Albion again promised to become a promotion force in the spring of 1974-75, only to hit the skids once more, starting with a 3-1 Easter Saturday defeat at Aston Villa. Albion led through Tony Brown at the break but were swept aside by this and two other second-half goals. Looking on in anguish for a side who parted company with Don Howe shortly afterwards are (from left) Gordon Nisbet, David Rushbury, Ian Edwards, Trevor Thompson and John Wile.

The Giles Revolution

Johnny Giles was appointed in July, 1975, as Albion's first player-manager but early results were not encouraging. A 1-0 home victory over Luton was his side's only win in the first ten League games, the eighth of which was this 1-1 draw at Alan Ashman's Carlisle. John Osborne's handling is tested here, with Geoff Hurst ducking and Trevor Thompson, Alistair Robertson and John Wile keeping a close eye. Ally Brown scored Albion's goal in front of a crowd well below 7,000. Picture courtesy of Carlisle Evening News.

Joe Mayo guides in an early header to put Albion ahead on their crucial trip to Bolton on November 29, 1975. Although Roy Greaves equalised in a game shown on that night's Match of the Day, a late shot by Bryan Robson (also pictured here) ended Bolton's run of 16 games without defeat. Improving Albion were sixth after this fourth win in five League matches and had come through with flying colours from a demanding trot of five away fixtures in six.

Ally Brown can't quite force the ball home in Albion's exciting fourth-round FA Cup victory over Graham Taylor's Lincoln on January 24, 1976. Goals by Tony Brown, Mick Martin and Bryan Robson eventually saw them home 3-2 against a Fourth Division side who contained ex-Hawthorns duo Percy Freeman and Dick Krzywicki, plus John Ward, who was Taylor's subsequent managerial assistant. Albion lost heavily in a replay at Southampton in the next round.

Life was fun under Albion's first player-boss - even in inclement weather. The genial Giles is joined on the training ground by (from left) Bryan Robson, Len Cantello and Ray Wilson, the last of whom was struggling with his knee and had already played what proved to be the last of his 284 matches for the club. Albion had just won successive League games at York and Chelsea and would kick February off by beating Bristol Rovers 3-0 at The Hawthorns.

A crucial three points in the making as Mick Martin (right) is congratulated by (from left) Joe Mayo, John Wile and Alistair Brown, not to mention a few exhuberant supporters, after opening the scoring with a 55th minute header against Nottingham Forest in Albion's last home game of 1975-76. Willie Johnston sealed a 2-0 win and Johnny Giles' side were two points clear of fourth-placed Bolton from one more game played. Albion had two away games to finish with - and things were very, very tense!

Images of two fraught London trips late in 1975-76. Left: Alistair Brown challenges in a Friday night clash at Charlton - a game Albion lost 2-1 despite Tony Brown's successful penalty. It left them outside the promotion places on goal difference with four games to go in the days before teams had the play-offs as a safety net. But they then beat Fulham and Forest at home before drawing 0-0 at Orient in their penultimate game, John Wile contesting possession at Brisbane Road (right) with Tony Grealish - later to serve at The Hawthorns himself. Bolton lost at leaders Sunderland the same night to leave Albion knowing a last-afternoon win at Oldham would see them up.

FOREVER ALBION

John Osborne produces a safe catch in the pressure cooker atmosphere of Oldham's Boundary Park on the last afternoon of the Second Division promotion race on April 24, 1976. The ever-present keeper was such a bundle of nerves as he stepped off the coach before kick-off that he couldn't speak to well-wishers but he was his normal dependable self in keeping a 22nd League clean sheet of the season and underlining the feat as a club record. Ex-Albion striker David Shaw is the player denied here, under the gaze of Alistair Robertson, Mick Martin and a massive bank of Albion fans at the Radcliffe Road End of the ground. Tony Brown's 58th minute volley gave Johnny Giles' men a 1-0 victory - and promotion along with Sunderland and Bristol City to the exclusion of Bolton, who won 4-0 at Charlton on the last day.

WBA could well have stood for We're Back Again when Albion played a friendly at Villa six days after regaining their top-flight place. Typically, Willie Johnston, behind skipper John Wile, was happy to milk the moment amid a sporting guard of honour from their opponents. The Baggies' mood was further improved by a 1-0 win in a game serving as a testimonial for Villa's Fred Turnbull and in which keeper John Osborne briefly played outfield.

A nice little jolly! Tony Brown, John Wile, Len Cantello and Bryan Robson made a post-promotion trip to Dublin in early May, 1976, to support a testimonial fixture for Johnny Giles in the city of his birth. Also part of the Hawthorns delegation were receptionist Janet Simpson, long-serving chairman Bert Millichip and Giles' secretary Linda Evans. The popular player-manager resigned that summer over dissatisfaction with his role but was persuaded to stay on for one more year as the club tried to find their feet again among the elite.

Johnny Giles, followed down the tunnel by Willie Johnston and Mick Martin, leads Albion back into top-flight combat on August 21, 1976. Appropriately for the Irishman, the game was away to his former club Leeds - and the 1974 champions and 1975 European Cup finalists were thankful to escape with a 2-2 draw thanks to a late equaliser after the two Browns, Alistair and Tony, had established clear daylight between the sides.

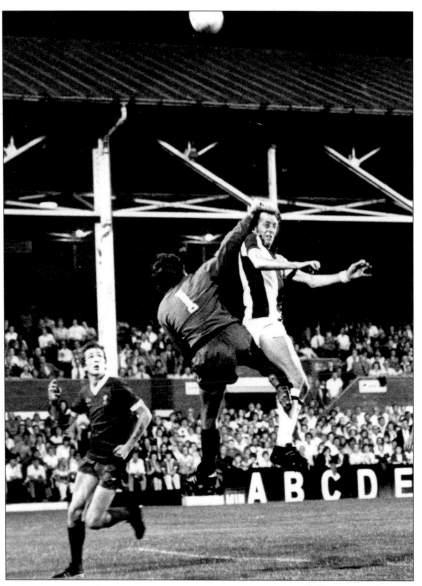

Mick Martin takes a painful punch from Liverpool keeper Ray Clemence on August 25, 1976, during Albion's first home game in the First Division for almost three and a half years. The skilful midfielder was an integral part of the possession game developed by Johnny Giles and, in 115 Baggies appearances, showed the form that brought him 52 Republic of Ireland caps. Alas, he couldn't stave off a 1-0 defeat here against the defending League champions.

Alistair Robertson boots clear from Scottish international Kenny Burns in the game at Birmingham watched by 38,448 on September 11, 1976. Following a mixed start, Albion were getting the hang of top-flight football, a fine goal by Tony Brown (pictured on the left) giving them a 1-0 victory - their first on the road since promotion - at a ground where they had said farewell to the First Division in 1973 and where they hadn't won since 1963-64.

Ray Treacy, the latest part of a sizeable Hawthorns-based Republic of Ireland contingent also containing Paddy Mulligan, Mick Martin and player-boss Johnny Giles, celebrates one of his two first-half goals in the 2-2 draw at Derby on September, 25, 1976. It was the striker's second debut for a club for whom he had also served in the mid-1960s - and he had scored in his first game back then, too! His two stints, though, brought him a total of only 28 games.

Bryan Robson crashes a shot past Dave Latchford in Albion's 2-1 League win at home to Birmingham on February 28, 1977. Ally Brown was also on target as the team embarked on a run of five successive First Division victories following a nightmare 6-1 crash at Sunderland. It was one of nine goals the brilliant Robson scored in season 1976-77 despite breaking his leg three times. The grounded Blues defender is Gary Emmanuel.

John Osborne peers from afar as Paddy Mulligan jostles with John O'Hare and Charlie George in Albion's 1-0 home victory over Derby on March 5, 1977. Bryan Robson scored for a side who were suddenly in rich form, their subsequent success at Tottenham being marked by debuts for Tony Godden and Laurie Cunningham. Osborne was to play the last of his 312 games for the club a few weeks later.

Derek Statham is helpless as Martin Dobson glances home a header to peg Albion back in a 1-1 draw at Everton in May, 1976. It was Johnny Giles' last but one match before calling it a day as manager and he steered Albion to a highly creditable final placing of seventh in the table. In the background are Willie Johnston and Everton's Mick Lyons. Tony Brown had given the visitors the lead.

Allen's Prize Legacy

A new face exploded on to the Hawthorns scene early in 1977-78. Cyrille Regis was captured by Ronnie Allen for £5,000 from non-League Hayes and quickly made his mark with this goal - and another from a penalty - on his debut in a 4-0 League Cup slaughter of Rotherham on August 31. With his raw pace and power, the striker instantly became a crowd favourite and struck with the first of his trademark spectacular goals during the follow-up League victory at home to Middlesbrough, a tussle from which is captured below. Regis clearly had the knack for making a quick impact. He scored in his first game for Albion in five different competitions.

After his excellent League debut, Regis scored again the following weekend, not that the 3-0 victory at Newcastle was just about one man. Albion were outstanding and Laurie Cunningham, above, and Bryan Robson were also on target to underline their supremacy. Mike Mahoney is the floundering goalkeeper and Micky Burns the man tracking back as the visitors moved up among the early pacesetters. Albion have not won in the League at St James' Park in nearly 30 years since.

Left: Another sign of Albion mastery of Newcastle in the same game as keeper Tony Godden advances and makes a safe catch, with support at his side from the dependable Alistair Robertson.

Goals flowed in the first three months of Albion's 1977-78 campaign, rarely more so than in this entertaining 3-3 draw at West Ham on November 12. David Cross, pictured here trying to get on the end of a cross, didn't score against a club he would later serve for three years but John Wile (right) netted twice and Laurie Cunningham once to keep the side flying high. Also in shot is Bryan Robson, whose Hammers namesake is on the right in the background.

A shocker of a night out! Albion had impressively drawn 0-0 in the League at champions-to-be Nottingham Forest three days earlier but that proved no insurance against this nightmare 1-0 League Cup fourth-round exit at Third Division Bury on November 29, 1977. A tangle between David Cross and Billy Tucker brought no joy and Albion couldn't get out of frozen, foggy Gigg Lane quickly enough at the end. Bury lost 3-0 to Forest in the next round.

Alistair Robertson, watched by Len Cantello, hurtles into a challenge in a best-forgotten derby clash at Aston Villa on December 10, 1977. Albion lost 3-0 and had suddenly gone five matches without scoring, their fine start to the season rapidly becoming a thing of the past. Cantello didn't play again after this game for four months, by which time a new man was in charge at The Hawthorns.

Three days before Christmas, 1977, following a home win over West Ham, Hawthorns legend Ronnie Allen packed his bags to become national coach in Saudi Arabia. He later managed Panathinaikos before returning for another spell at Albion. Taking centre stage at the farewell niceties is 'hoodie' Willie Johnston (second right) while skipper John Wile extends a handshake shortly before he and physio George Wright took caretaker control.

The Mauling of Man Utd

(Part Two)

Alistair Brown falls while heading Albion's second goal in their stunning 4-0 home win over United on October 16, 1976. Alex Stepney is the keeper and Jimmy Nicholl (later of Albion) looks on, Johnny Giles' men hitting four for a second home game running after coming from 2-0 down to beat Spurs. Johnny Giles, Len Cantello and Ray Treacy also scored against United before the Match of the Day cameras.

Beating United 4-0 was special; to repeat the feat a year later confirmed why the Red Devils came to dread visits to Albion. Laurie Cunningham, socks rolled down as usual, beats Alex Stepney (above) for one of the goals in the follow-up rout on October 22, 1977. Below: Tony Brown and Paddy Mulligan see David Cross sidefoot the second of his two goals in a game in which John Wile also hit the target against the FA Cup holders. It wasn't just at home that Albion made life hard for United. At Old Trafford, they drew in the League in 1976-77 and 1977-78 and won there spectacularly in 1978-79 as well as drawing in the 1977-78 FA Cup.

More United pain in a dream FA Cup round-four replay on February 1, 1978. Albion were held up by Steve Coppell's last-gasp equaliser at Old Trafford but this replay was a classic. No-one enjoyed it more than Cyrille Regis, who scored twice in the rain, hitting the winner (above) early in extra-time after Ally Brown hit the bar. Arthur Albiston's slide can't prevent the ball beating Alex Stepney (below) as Brown celebrates and Stewart Houston (left) and Martin Buchan flounder. Tony Brown had put Ron Atkinson's Albion on their way to a 3-2 success in a tie in which John Wile went off with a facial injury after a controversial Joe Jordan challenge.

Another incisive Albion blow in the Cup conquest of United in February, 1978…..Regis puts away a header to make it 2-1 after a Willie Johnston piledriver had struck the bar. The striker quickly sensed his chance despite the presence of Jimmy Nicholl and goalkeeper Stepney. It was a massive scalp given that United had overcome Liverpool in the previous season's Wembley final and had lost only once in 18 FA Cup ties.

Albion again made light work of United in 1982-83. Above: Martyn Bennett, who scored only ten times in 217 first-team games for the club, rises to direct a header goalwards despite the proximity of Kevin Moran and no 4 Ray Wilkins. Below: Job done! Bennett and Ally Robertson punch the air in delight at the equaliser as Gordon McQueen starts the inquest with keeper Gary Bailey. Albion had lost 3-0 at home to United in 1981-82 but this 3-1 win, including further goals by Peter Eastoe and Ally Brown, meant they had beaten them seven times out of eight at home since 1976, scoring 20 goals in the process. They defeated them again at The Hawthorns in 1983-84.

Big Ron, Big Ambitions

Continuing the exciting dawn to the Big Ron Era…..Albion had already ko'd Blackpool and Manchester United when they registered this thrilling FA Cup fifth-round win at Derby on February 23, 1978. The first of no 9 Cyrille Regis' brace is looming here (above) as Alistair Brown heads across the six-yard area. Willie Johnston netted the other goal. The little-known Atkinson had arrived from Cambridge in mid-January and was all smiles in the dressing room afterwards as he quenched his thirst with Alistair Robertson and keeper Tony Godden. It was Albion's only post-war victory at the Baseball Ground but League fortunes initially remained modest under the new regime. The first ten Division One games the club played in 1978 yielded only one win - at Birmingham on Brendon Batson's debut.

Albion really had the FA cup bit between their teeth when they put Nottingham Forest to flight in round six at The Hawthorns in March, 1978. Brian Clough's champions-elect were a supremely dominant side at the time and, remarkably, this was their only defeat in 62 games in League and cups, their historic sequence of 42 First Division games unbeaten already well advanced. Ally Brown fails to find a way past Peter Shilton here but Mick Martin and Cyrille Regis did in a 2-0 victory.

Left: Albion's 18th appearance in the semi-final of the FA Cup was an unhappy one. Warm favourites to beat Bobby Robson's Ipswich, they lost 3-1 at Highbury, with John Wile having to go off with a gash suffered in an early clash of heads as Brian Talbot opened the scoring. From left, Paul Cooper, Talbot, Mick Mills, Wile, Albion scorer Tony Brown and Allan Hunter are pictured in a tie which saw Mick Martin sent off.

Below: Manchester-born Len Cantello seems to be receiving a bite from Gary Owen in Albion's 3-1 League win at Maine Road on April 15, 1978. Cyrille Regis, Laurie Cunningham and Alistair Brown scored in the club's fifth away League victory of the season and Owen moved to Albion in 1979, becoming a replacement for Cantello, who headed for Bolton in the same summer after 369 Baggies matches.

Close escape for Derby but they didn't emerge unscathed from their visit to The Hawthorns on April 18, 1978. Tony Brown, getting back to his feet in the six-yard area as a loose ball just evades Alistair Brown, scored the only goal from a second-half penalty and Albion had registered five League victories in a row, three of them straight after their FA Cup semi-final heartbreak. The Derby trio (from left) are John Middleton, Roy McFarland and Colin Todd.

Wayne Hughes, a Welshman who captained Albion to 1976 FA Youth Cup glory, sidefoots the second goal in a 2-2 home draw with champions Nottingham Forest on the last day of 1977-78. The point, also arising from Tony Brown's 23rd goal of the season, proved enough to secure Albion's qualification for Europe for the first time in ten years. Cyrille Regis, having just hit the bar with a header, shouts his delight as Forest's defenders despair.

Despite a long close-season trip to China and Hong Kong, Albion started 1978-79 brilliantly with single-goal successes at home to Ipswich and at QPR, then this crushing of newly-promoted Bolton. The 4-0 romp was set up by goals by Alistair Brown (2), Laurie Cunningham and Cyrille Regis, Cunningham and Bryan Robson doing their best to engineer another here until Tony Dunne boots clear.

Despite a surprise first defeat of the season at Derby, Albion were still very much on the boil by the time they crossed swords at The Hawthorns with a Liverpool side who had won the European Cup for the previous two years. Ron Atkinson's team excelled once more, Laurie Cunningham bamboozling Emlyn Hughes and Ray Clemence to open the scoring with this fine solo effort before Kenny Dalglish rescued a point after a famous Tony Godden howler.

Ally Brown is denied in the League Cup round-two second replay against Leeds in October, 1978. After two 0-0 draws, Albion lost by the only goal at Maine Road and had Len Cantello sent off. Tony Brown, looking on with Bryan Robson, Byron Stevenson and Brian Flynn, equalled Ronnie Allen's club record of 208 League goals by scoring in a 3-1 win at Chelsea two days earlier, and passed Allen's mark at Leeds within a fortnight - one of an incredible seven meetings of the clubs that season in the League, League Cup and FA Cup.

Alistair Brown turns defender to preserve Albion's clean sheet on their League visit to Bolton only three days before they set off to Spain for their UEFA Cup clash in Valencia. This soggy clash, on November 18, 1978, brought a third successive win in the League and a fifth in six Division One games, the only goal coming, like at Ipswich seven days earlier, from Brown. Photograph courtesy of Bolton Evening News.

Albion returned home from their heroic 1-1 draw in Valencia to face Villa in the League only three days later - and their star appeared to be rising even further when Tony Brown bludgeoned this first-half penalty past Jimmy Rimmer for one of his 51 successful spot-kicks. Travel weariness perhaps told in the second half, though, because Villa equalised through Allan Evans and departed with a draw.

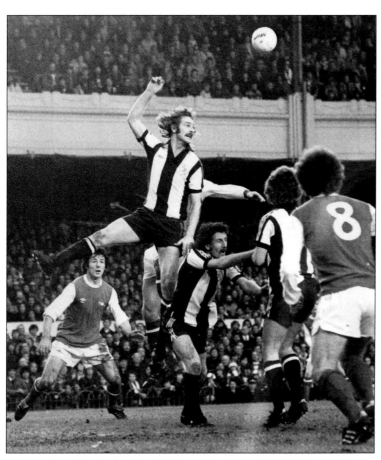

One of the high spots of Albion's excellent 1978-79 season.....a 2-1 Boxing Day victory at Arsenal. Bryan Robson, partly obscured by no 8 Alan Sunderland (above left), and Alistair Brown soon had the Gunners two down, then the likes of Alistair Robertson, pictured leaving Frank Stapleton grounded, helped underpin the club's fourth win in a run of six that included the memorable 5-3 triumph against Manchester United at Old Trafford on December 30. Above right: John Wile climbs highest to head clear at Highbury.

Albion were really looking the part as title challengers when, clad in their famous snow boots, they had Bristol City slipping and sliding to defeat on New Year's Day, 1979. Cyrille Regis did not manage to add to his tally of 12 goals for the season but Alistair Brown scored twice to join him in double figures and John Wile once to set Ron Atkinson's team up to climb to the Championship summit with a 1-1 draw 12 days later at Norwich, where Regis was on target.

Laurie Cunningham cuts in but fails to ruffle Liverpool's cast-iron defence in the decisive second v first clash on February 3, 1979. Albion travelled to Anfield as leaders, only for a three-week break enforced by heavy snow to check their momentum. Liverpool, saved from such rustiness by being able to play in the meantime, won this game 2-1, the goal they conceded to Ally Brown at 2-0 proving to be one of only four they conceded at home in the League that season in surging to their third League title in four years.

Derek Statham watches Southampton go close in a 1-1 FA Cup fifth-round draw on March 10, 1979. Tony Godden, Brendon Batson and John Wile also look on in a tie in which Ally Brown levelled. Albion, having hammered Coventry 4-0 in the third round then beaten Leeds 2-0 in a second replay in round four, bowed out 2-1 at The Dell in extra-time despite a Laurie Cunningham goal and this advance (below) by the two Browns and Ally Robertson. Games came thick and fast after part two of the big freeze, which saw Albion go another three weeks without a League game after the trip to Anfield. Albion's UEFA Cup quarter-final away leg against Red Star Belgrade came three days before the home tie against the Saints, then they played eight games in March, eight in April and six from May 1 to May 18.

FOREVER ALBION

David Mills became Great Britain's priciest footballer when Albion paid £500,000 for him in the mid-winter of 1978-79. Having excelled at Middlesbrough, though, he failed at The Hawthorns as a potential replacement for the ageing Tony Brown. Mills is seen here trying to turn Alan Ramage in a 1-1 draw away to his old club Boro on April 28, 1979 - a fixture in which Alistair Brown (pictured to the left) netted the last but one of the 24 goals that made him Albion's top scorer during the season.

Albion finished an unflattering third in 1978-79, pipped to runners-up spot by Nottingham Forest via a late goal in the West Midlands v East Midlands showdown at The Hawthorns in the final game. Despite Laurie Cunningham's subsequent £1m sale to Real Madrid and Len Cantello's move to Bolton, hopes were high for Albion's 1979-80 centenary season - preceded by a 1-0 win in this prestige friendly at home to Ajax, new signing Peter Barnes (background left) scoring the goal.

A Funny Thing Happened...

Canine capers at The Hawthorns as play in an Albion v Liverpool top-flight game in November, 1968, is halted by a black mongrel. Alun Evans stoops to try to try to persuade the enthusiastic invader to take an early bath while Bobby Hope and Roger Hunt (with ball) settle for spectators' roles. The clash ended 0-0, FA Cup holders Albion having held League champions-elect Leeds by the same score at Elland Road the previous Saturday.

Left: Everton's Dave Jones struggles to keep up with Albion trio Jack Russell, Alistair Brown and Mick Martin in a 3-0 home win at The Hawthorns on November 27, 1976. The tiny terrier proved himself a real box-to-box performer and harassed the Merseysiders' defenders shortly afterwards into losing their concentration and allowing David Cross - making his home debut after being signed from Coventry - to nip in and beat keeper Dai Davies for goal no 2.

Left: Part one of the strange career of Gordon Nisbet! The Geordie leads Alan Merrick, Graham Lovett and Jim Holton out for a reserve game as he starts football life as a goalkeeper. He made his senior Albion debut in goal in a 3-1 defeat at Coventry in August, 1969, but quickly decided outfield duties suited him better and went on to play 166 games as the club's right-back. Nisbet later took his haul of career League appearances to 620 with stints at Hull, Plymouth and Exeter.

Below: Drop it on my toe, bro! Peter Latchford is confronted by his older brother Bob in his second senior game in Albion's goal in a 2-2 Hawthorns draw with newly-promoted Birmingham on August 30, 1972. There may have been a third family member on view but Mike Kelly, not Dave Latchford, was Blues' keeper. Lyndon Hughes, Ray Wilson and no 2 Gordon Nisbet are the other Albion players on a night when Bobby Hope was in the visitors' line-up.

Looking like Leeds in appearance only….Albion didn't have a suitable change kit when they arrived at Elland Road on the second Saturday of 1972-73 and had to don their hosts' yellow and blue second strip. The look didn't lift them, though, with boyhood Baggies fan Allan Clarke leaving Graham Smith helpless here in the keeper's penultimate game for the club with the first of his two goals. League champions Leeds won 2-0 and Albion had to wait for their fourth game - a 1-1 midweek draw at Newcastle - for their first goal.

Another unscheduled change….. John Wile, in Shrewsbury's red and white second colours because both of Albion's two strips were unsuitable, celebrates in the League Cup second-round first leg at the Gay Meadow on October 6, 1981. Against a side containing Bernard McNally, Albion led 3-0 in 31 minutes through Cyrille Regis, Steve Mackenzie and Nicky Cross, only for the Second Division side to draw 3-3 and then lose only 2-1 in the second leg.

Gary Owen hails his first minute goal against Nottingham Forest on September 1, 1979 - his first since a £465,000 move from Manchester City that summer. The breakthrough was engineered by Kevin Summerfield, the no 8 making his first League start for the club. But Albion, with only one point from their previous three matches, proceeded to cave in to the European champions, who ran out 5-1 winners.

John Wile clears from Bolton's Alan Gowling in a 0-0 draw at Burnden Park on September 8, 1979, as Alistair Robertson waits for any slips. The white-shirted player to the right is ex-Albion midfielder Len Cantello, who had moved north in the summer. Ron Atkinson's side made a poor start after their 1978-79 heroics, losing three and drawing two of their opening five League games. Picture courtesy of the Bolton Evening News.

With Willie Johnston leaving in 1979 after his eclipse by Laurie Cunningham, Peter Barnes had a prolific debut season on Albion's left wing. He scored the club's first goal of 1979-80 and would add a further 14, including a brace at Highfield Road in the second leg of a League double over Coventry. Here, he torments Mick Coop in the 2-1 League Cup win at home to the Sky Blues on September 26, Albion losing at Norwich in the next round.

John Trewick, a member of Albion's victorious 1976 FA Youth Cup winning team, keeps his feet while Steve Perryman (left) and Glenn Hoddle go to ground in the clash at Tottenham in late September, 1979. The 1-1 draw was secured by Alistair Brown's late goal and was further marked by the Baggies debut of John Deehan. Albion had thrashed Manchester City 4-0 on the previous Saturday.

Treatment for Derek Statham, already with over 100 top-flight appearances to his name, in the 3-0 League Cup fourth-round replay defeat at Norwich on November 7. The left-back didn't play again for several weeks because of knee ligament damage and then faced a longer lay-off through injury. Albion's unhappy start to the season had contained a nightmare UEFA Cup first-stage exit against Carl Zeiss Jena.

Another goal for Peter Barnes, this time from the penalty spot on a December 8 League trip to Stoke. Note the actions of John Wile, who appears to be looking to the bench for confirmation of whether or not keeper Roger Jones has been beaten. Also looking on are (from left) Brendon Batson, Alistair Brown and David Mills. Cyrille Regis and Barnes hauled Albion back level, only for Garth Crooks - later to be recruited to The Hawthorns - to complete his hat-trick and earn Stoke a 3-2 victory.

Ipswich survive this powerful effort by Bryan Robson at Portman Road on the first day of the 1980s. Mick Mills, John Wark and Russell Osman are the covering opponents and John Deehan is in the background on an afternoon when Tony Brown made his last League start for the Baggies - at the ground where he made his debut as a 17-year-old in 1963. This wasn't a happy occasion, Albion losing 4-0, their second of three successive defeats.

Partly-hidden Ally Robertson powers a header past Ally Brown and no 3 Kenny Sansom to start Albion's revival in a 2-2 draw at Crystal Palace on January 26, 1980. Ron Atkinson's side were two down but rallied and levelled through Cyrille Regis, having recently gone out of the FA Cup on another trip to London with a 3-1 third-round replay defeat at West Ham. John Deehan is on the left.

Peter Barnes arrows in one of the two goals that made his return trip to Maine Road on February 2, 1980, a happy occasion. The talented left-winger, capped 22 times by England, set up a 3-1 victory - the club's first since the same player had contributed a brace to a 3-0 Boxing Day home win over Bristol City seven games earlier. Another ex-Manchester City player, Gary Owen, is on the left. Cyrille Regis scored Albion's other goal on this rain-lashed afternoon.

A happy 22nd birthday for Cyrille Regis on February 9, 1980, as he touches home one of his and Albion's two goals in a narrow home win over Tottenham, the club he supported as a boy. It took the striker's scoring haul to five in four League matches and he would finish with nine League and cup goals in a season in which injury prevented him starting a First Division game until the end of November. Ally Brown and John Wile prepare to celebrate amid Spurs' protests for an infringement.

Cyrille Regis fails to find the target in the clash of two Albions at a newly-promoted Brighton on February 16, 1980. Martyn Bennett and Alistair Brown are the other Baggies players in the picture while the moustachioed home man just to the right of the ball is Mark Lawrenson. This was Albion's first-ever League or cup outing at the now built-upon Goldstone Ground - and finished 0-0.

Above: Joy for John Deehan as Peter Barnes puts Albion on course for a third successive Highfield Road win on March 8, 1980. Barnes also scored from a penalty to secure a 3-1 victory against a side they beat 4-1 in the League and 2-1 in the League Cup at The Hawthorns earlier in the season. Below: Another win in the making as Brendon Batson slices through Leeds' defence on March 29, 1980, to tee up John Deehan for one of only three goals he managed in his debut season at the club. Peter Barnes (penalty) was also on target for a team then on a run of only one defeat in 17 League games, although they finished tenth as a modest follow-up to the previous season's heights.

FOREVER ALBION

Peter Barnes shrugs off some dubious attention to accelerate for goal in Albion's 2-1 victory at Brighton on August 30, 1980. It was a first League success of the season for the Baggies following a poor, low-scoring start in which they had lost at home to Arsenal and drawn both at Stoke and in the derby with Wolves at The Hawthorns. They were also in a spot of bother at the Goldstone Ground for a while before recovering from one down to win with efforts from Cyrille Regis and Gary Owen.

Cyrille Regis didn't succeed with this header but hit a late clincher in the League Cup round-two return at Leicester on September 3, 1980. Albion had also won by the only goal in the first leg at home - scored by Peter Barnes - and were on a run of four consecutive victories. The Foxes proved to be meat and drink to them that season, also suffering a League double at their hands. Other Albion men pictured are (from left) Gary Owen, Ally Brown and Ally Robertson.

Cyrille Regis stands aside to allow Alistair Brown through to sweep his right-foot shot past Kevin Bond for his first goal of 1980-81 - in the 3-0 early-September home victory over Norwich. The ex-Manchester City duo of Peter Barnes (penalty) and Gary Owen were also on target, although Atkinson's men caught a cold in their next fixture by losing 4-0 at League champions Liverpool. Brown and Regis were to score steadily throughout the season.

Another goal for Ally Brown, this time in the 1-1 draw at Birmingham on September 20, 1980. Peter Barnes is up in support with the striker - by now the only Brown at The Hawthorns - while Mark Dennis and keeper Jeff Wealands are powerless to intervene. Albion remained on the boil by winning 2-1 in the third round of the League Cup at Everton four nights later and then returning home to beat Southampton with a Brown brace.

Proud moment for Bryan Robson in the late autumn of 1980 - the year in which he was named as Midland Footballer of the Year and Midland Sportswriters' Player of the Year. In 1979, he was chosen as Sports Argus-Sportsco Footballer of the Year and, despite being only 23 at the time of this hand-over by Bert Millichip, Albion's chairman for many years, had already played well over 160 games for the club.

Big smiles from John Trewick (left) and Cyrille Regis after the latter opened the scoring in the 3-1 win over Manchester City at The Hawthorns on October 11, 1980 - Albion's fourth successive League victory. Trewick was on target himself along with Bryan Robson, a fellow Geordie with whom he came through the Baggies ranks. This was one of the last of Trewick's 134 games for the club before joining Newcastle. City's no 1 is Joe Corrigan, in much more recent times a Baggies goalkeeper coach.

Skipper John Wile savours his equaliser in Albion's 1-1 First Division draw at Everton on October 21, 1980. Cyrille Regis waits to join in the celebrations while the home no 10 is Asa Hartford, a Hawthorns team-mate of Wile's until 1974. Albion had won at Goodison Park in the League Cup a few weeks earlier on the night director Tom Silk was killed in a plane crash on his way to Merseyside from France.

Cyrille Regis grew to love his trips with Albion to Crystal Palace. He scored one of the goals on the day they rescued a top-flight point at Selhurst Park in 1979-80 and went one better when netting twice in a League Cup triumph there in 1981-82. In between, he found the net just once but it was the match-winner in this League visit in early October, 1980. Paul Barron is the home goalkeeper.

Albion keeper Tony Godden had played more than 140 consecutive League matches come the day of this 0-0 home draw with Villa on November 8, 1980. All told, he would appear in 228 senior matches in a row and was a League ever-present for four seasons running. Gary Owen, Ally Robertson, Remi Moses, the grounded Barry Cowdrill, John Wile, Bryan Robson and Brendon Batson help him to see off this attack, led by Peter Withe and Gordon Cowans.

FOREVER ALBION

Albion, with John Wile leading the threat to Mark Wallington's goal, were still in fine form when they recorded this 3-1 home win over Leicester on November 22, 1980. Goals by Bryan Robson, Remi Moses and Gary Owen (penalty) saw them home at a time when they had lost only once in 16 League and League Cup matches. In the later competition, they had needed three tries to beat Preston and would then be edged out at Manchester City in round five.

Rarely did Ayresome Park bring Albion any joy and this trip to the north-east on January 24, 1981, was no exception as it spelled the end of the FA Cup road for another season. Martyn Bennett bullets a header off target, watched by Bryan Robson (left) and Alistair Brown on an afternoon when Middlesbrough came up with only goal of the tie. Albion had overpowered Second Division Grimsby 3-0 at The Hawthorns in the previous round.

Delight for Remi Moses after he had left defender Joe Gallagher flatfooted on the line to give Albion a fifth minute lead in their derby at home to Birmingham on February 28, 1981. Alistair Brown was also among the scorers but Blues hit back to force the second of four successive League draws between the clubs. Bryan Robson is also pictured here. The attendance was only 24,843 - disappointing for a club who were challenging for a place in Europe.

Bryan Robson and Remi Moses at the heart of the action once more, with Robson this time taking centre stage by firing home 90 seconds from the end for the only goal of the game against Crystal Palace at The Hawthorns on March 7, 1981. It was one of ten League goals the brilliant midfielder scored that season and, overall in all competitions, he would score 46 times in 249 appearances for the club. Alistair Brown is the no 8 looking on approvingly.

Brendon Batson flings himself bravely across the path of Terry Butcher to head one of only two goals he managed in no fewer than 220 Albion appearances spanning five years. The stylish right-back, later to serve as the club's managing director, also scored in a 1978-79 FA Cup slaughter of Coventry and helped the club into the UEFA Cup (via an excellent final placing of fourth) with this 3-1 early-April victory at home to title-chasing Ipswich.

New season, same drill.....Cyrille Regis, leading scorer in 1980-81 with 17 goals, nets the second of his three in a 4-1 home win over top-flight newcomers Swansea on September 5, 1981. Steve Mackenzie was also on target but Albion failed to score in their next five games, including the away leg of their UEFA Cup tie against Grasshoppers Zurich. Swansea emerged as a surprise force in their first season up and were to finish in the more than healthy position of sixth.

End Of A Golden Era

Gary Owen is out of luck with this lob in Albion's 0-0 draw at Nottingham Forest on September 12, 1981. Cyrille Regis looks on from behind him while Remi Moses (far left) was playing the last of his 63 League matches for the club, although he also figured in the UEFA Cup trip to Switzerland four days later. Albion won 2-1 in the Hawthorns return against 1979 and 1980 European champions Forest in the New Year but, with Ron Atkinson having departed for Manchester United in summer, 1981, further big changes were on the way......

Albion's unhappy 1-0 defeat at Everton on September 26, 1981, was Bryan Robson's last game before he and Remi Moses rejoined Ron Atkinson by making a £2m joint switch to Manchester United. Robson, valued at £1.5m, so became the country's costliest player. Brendon Batson and Cyrille Regis keep a close watch here on Mike Pejic in a game in which Albion - by now under the management of Ronnie Allen for the second time - gave a League debut to former Goodison midfielder Andy King.

Albion had won only one of their opening 11 First Division matches when they made the short trip to St Andrew's on October 31, 1981. And even Cyrille Regis's second hat-trick of the season failed to bring them maximum points, Birmingham hitting back from 3-1 down to draw 3-3. Brendon Batson is the team-mate playing a hand in the second goal here, the striker being pursued by Kevan Broadhurst as he drives past keeper Jeff Wealands.

Albion may have been languishing in the League but they impressed in the cups in 1981-82. Having narrowly beaten Shrewsbury at the first stage of the League Cup, they contested a third-round marathon with West Ham that was all about Cyrille Regis. The powerful striker outpaced Alvin Martin (above) to beat Phil Parkes and help give his side a 2-0 lead in the original tie at Upton Park on November 10. They were pegged back, though, and then held 1-1 at The Hawthorns despite extra-time in the replay. West Ham won the toss to stage the second replay and almost 25,000 saw the deadlock broken only seven minutes from the end (below) by Regis, who held off Billy Bonds to shoot past Parkes. The win was all the more worthy as Albion had Ally Brown sent off.

Second Division Crystal Palace suffer this time as Cyrille Regis beats keeper Paul Barron - later to play for Albion - in a League Cup fourth-round tie at Selhurst Park. The striker scored two in this 3-1 victory to take his season's tally to 17 by mid-December. The Baggies' other goal in their fourth straight win came from Derek Monaghan (left). Mickey Lewis, at 16 years ten months, went on as substitute to become the youngest player to serve Albion in the League Cup.

Derek Statham had scored only once in more than five years for Albion up to January, 1982, since his memorable debut-day goal past Peter Shilton at Stoke in December, 1976. That second effort came at home to Coventry in a 7-1 rout in 1978-79. In the space of four days, though, he netted two more, including the winner in Albion's 1-0 FA Cup fourth-round victory at Third Division Gillingham, where he also found himself the centre of some questionable attention here.

Above: Delight for Derek Statham with a winner at the Villa! Albion's attack-minded left-back pops up deep in home territory to settle this League Cup quarter-final meeting on January 20, 1982, with the only goal. Andy King savours the moment, too, as Jimmy Rimmer and Gary Williams are left despairing. It was a sizeable scalp for Albion despite their opponents being reduced to ten men by Tony Morley's sending-off. League champions Villa, at the time, were on their way to winning the European Cup. Below: Statham is in the thick of the action as he boots clear deep in the second half, watched by (from left) Gary Owen, John Wile, a grounded Martin Jol and Brendon Batson.

Nearly Men Again

Two moments from the League Cup semi-final against Tottenham which might have helped send Albion to Wembley. Above: Derek Monaghan, watched by Cyrille Regis, is denied by a flying save from Ray Clemence in the goalless first leg at The Hawthorns on February 3, 1982 - a tie marred by the sendings-off of Martin Jol (now Spurs' manager) and Tony Galvin. Albion had a good enough record against the North London club to encourage them for the return trip to White Hart Lane a week later despite having to give young full-back David Arthur one of only six first-team appearances. They had won four and drawn two of their previous six matches against Spurs going back to 1979 and threatened here with a header from Alistair Robertson. But, as if to underline their tag as 'nearly men,' they slipped to a 1-0 defeat and it was Tottenham who went on to meet - and lose to - Liverpool in the final.

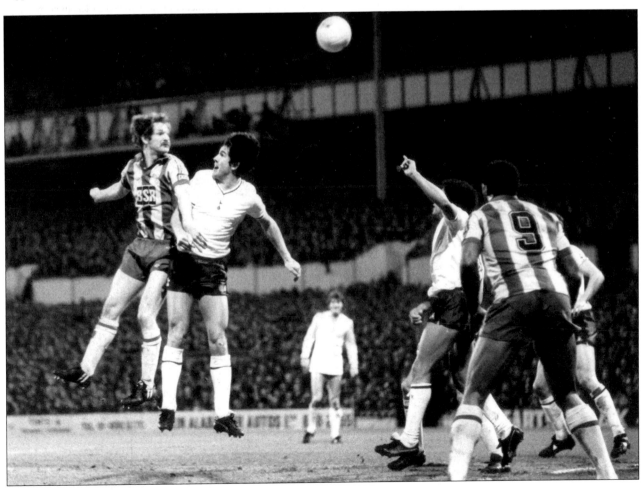

Albion were still comfortable in mid-table, having also beaten Blackburn as well as Gillingham in the FA Cup, by the time they registered this 2-1 home League victory over Nottingham Forest on February 6, 1982. The man wheeling away in celebration from Peter Shilton, Cyrille Regis, Viv Anderson and no 5 Willie Young is Kevin Summerfield, who has just scored what proved to be the winner. On the left, arm raised, is Clive Whitehead.

In the days when Albion frequently brought some points back from Arsenal, Martyn Bennett surges between Paul Davis and David O'Leary in the 2-2 midweek draw on March 16, 1982. Andy King and substitute Nicky Cross scored for a side who were in a run of five draws in six League matches. And Ronnie Allen's men would have a more important trip to Highbury a few weeks later....

Two shots of the game that propelled Albion into the FA Cup semi-finals for the 19th and latest time. Ronnie Allen's side could not have chosen more welcome visitors at the last-eight stage than their frequent whipping boys Coventry - and they made short work of them on a foul Hawthorns afternoon. Above: Cyrille Regis seems suspended in mid-air as he bludgeons home one of the goals by which Albion won 2-0, having beaten Norwich 1-0 (with yet another Regis blockbuster) at home in round five. David Barnes, Gary Gillespie and Danny Thomas, the latter a Baggies physio in more recent times, are the men tracking back in vain. Below: Martyn Bennett, already bedevilled by some of the injury problems that were to cut short a highly promising career, goes close to making it two as he shapes to shoot despite a tackle by Gillespie under Gerry Francis's watchful eye. Gary Owen eventually scored Albion's second.

Sheer pain for big Cyrille Regis. Above: The ever-popular striker lunges in front of QPR's ex-Wolves defender Bob Hazell to head just off target as Albion's FA Cup semi-final appearance in 1981-82 proves no happier than the one they made at the same stage of the League Cup a few weeks earlier. Ronnie Allen's side were hot favourites against their Second Division opponents and their shock 1967 Wembley conquerors - but an attempted clearance by the also-pictured Alistair Robertson rebounded fortuitously into the net off Clive Allen for the only goal deep in the second half. It was a defeat that Regis took badly after he also played in the semi-final KO by Ipswich at the same stadium in 1978 and he is clearly feeling the anguish as he is consoled by the Rangers duo of Peter Hucker (later to have a short spell with Albion) and Glenn Roeder. QPR lost to Tottenham in the final.

Albion In Europe

(Part Two)

Albion's first sortie into Europe for ten years got off to a scintillating start in September, 1978 - despite problems with their opening assignment against Galatasaray. The away leg was switched from Istanbul to the coastal city of Izmir because of earlier crowd trouble, then severe traffic meant Albion were late arriving at the Ataturk Stadium. But Bryan Robson still got them off to a flier with this seventh minute goal from close range which was followed by Laurie Cunningham's brace in a 3-1 victory.

John Trewick bears down on the Galatasaray goal during Albion's impressive progress through the second round of the 1978-79 UEFA Cup. The Turks escaped on this occasion, although the midfielder was on target in a 3-1 win, but were bundled out 6-2 on aggregate, with Laurie Cunningham (penalty) and Bryan Robson also scoring. Reserve keeper Mark Grew made his senior debut in this return when going on as substitute for Tony Godden.

Cyrille Regis turns away after scoring Albion's second goal in their 2-0 first-leg victory away to Sporting Braga in the UEFA Cup third round on October 18, 1978. The striker netted a brace in front of 31,000 in Portugal at a time he and the side were also bombing along in the League. He had just netted twice in a 3-1 win at Leeds and would do the same in a 7-1 Hawthorns humiliation of Coventry.

No slip-ups....Albion did what they had to do in the second leg against Braga, Laurie Cunningham threatening further damage as he gets to grips with an opponent here. Alistair Brown scored the only goal of this November 1 clash as Ron Atkinson's exhilarating side made it four victories out of four in the UEFA Cup at a time when they had also won six and drawn four of their opening 12 First Division fixtures, losing only to Derby and Tottenham.

The high spot of a wondrous evening that earned Laurie Cunningham a move to Real Madrid. The gifted forward hooks the equaliser past keeper Pereira in the first leg of the UEFA Cup fourth-round 1-1 draw in Valencia in November, 1978 - and returned to Spain for almost £1m seven months later as Albion's record sale. Cunningham, bought for only £100,000 by Johnny Giles from Orient in 1977, was quite brilliant in the Luis Casanova Stadium in what was probably the club's finest ever performance in European football. Albion, trailing to a first half Dario Felman goal, recovered superbly and might well have made it three wins in three away first legs, with Bryan Robson going close (below) with a shot that was cleared off the line as Cunningham waits to pick up any crumbs.

ADIOS VALENCIA

Not to worry.....despite failing to make their first-leg supremacy tell, Atkinson's men won the second leg 2-0 against a side containing Argentine legend Mario Kempes and West German star Rainer Bonhof. They were helped on their way by this early Tony Brown penalty, captured from an Evening Mail cutting. Brown also hit a superb second late on.

Tony Brown climbs above his marker to head down towards namesake Ally in the away first leg of Albion's UEFA Cup quarter-final tie against Red Star Belgrade on March 7, 1979. A tremendous free-kick by centre-forward Dusko Savic six minutes from time gave the Yugoslavs a 1-0 victory on a night on which Albion played to the biggest audience, a massive 95,300, that they have ever appeared in front of for a competitive game played anywhere other than at Wembley.

The night that broke Albion's UEFA Cup hearts. Try as they did in their quarter-final return against Red Star Belgrade, they couldn't quite turn round the 1-0 defeat they had suffered a fortnight earlier. They were given a first-half lead by Cyrille Regis but the Yugoslavs equalised with a deflected shot in the dying minutes and went through 2-1. Red Star beat Hertha Berlin in the semi-final but lost to Borussia Moenchengladbach in the final.

Gloom for Albion on their 1979-80 European travels. Third place in the table the previous May put them back in the UEFA Cup but, with Len Cantello and Laurie Cunningham sold, they performed poorly. David Mills challenges (above) in a first-leg 2-0 defeat away to Carl Zeiss Jena that Ron Atkinson called the worst 90 minutes he had seen from any side he had managed. In another incident from the trip to East Germany, Derek Statham is challenged from behind by his marker (below). Carl Zeiss then won 2-1 at The Hawthorns, where Alistair Brown was sent off shortly before half-time.

Highlights - or maybe that should be lowlights - from the last European tie Albion played. Grasshoppers Zurich were the opponents for this UEFA Cup first-round clash in September, 1981, with Ronnie Allen's side more than hopeful of going through. On a ground where the manager had made his England debut 29 years earlier, a 1-0 defeat in the first leg in Switzerland kept the door open. And it might have been more promising still had this shot by Alistair Robertson succeeded, with David Mills looking on optimistically (above). But their fortunes nosedived in the second leg with a 3-1 defeat that sent them tumbling out 4-1 on aggregate. Robertson scored the goal and this effort by John Deehan (below) threatened until it was blocked by the keeper. Albion have generally scored freely on their excursions into Europe but have managed only three goals in their last six matches in the UEFA Cup.

On The Slippery Slope

The rot was setting in by the time Albion lost 3-1 on April 6, 1982 on this, their first top-flight visit (right) to Swansea's Vetch Field. It was their third successive defeat, including the FA Cup semi-final, and they were beaten in their following five League matches as well to hurtle deep into relegation danger. Cyrille Regis and substitute Alistair Brown lead the charge but all the side managed was a Steve Mackenzie goal that proved no more than a consolation.

Below: A crucial penalty save by Tony Godden from Wayne Clarke in the big Black Country relegation battle in April, 1982. Albion had slipped alarmingly down the table in the second half of the season but there was to be a happy ending for them. They won this game 2-1 with goals by Cyrille Regis and Derek Monaghan and stopped up, while Wolves took the big drop. Godden was back in favour, making his first League appearance for six months.

Derek Statham weaves between two Stoke defenders back at the ground where he made a scoring debut five seasons earlier. This Potteries trip on May 21, 1982, brought a 3-0 home win that narrowly preserved Stoke's top-flight status on the evening Denis Smith - later to manage Albion - played the last of his 493 games for them and Ronnie Allen signed off as Baggies boss. As a result, Leeds went down, having lost at The Hawthorns 48 hours earlier on a night when their fans rioted disgracefully at the Smethwick End.

Dark-haired Darren Edwards, with cousin Paul, finds himself in distinguished company on September 1, 1982 as a pick-me-up following a knee operation. The young duo's Hawthorns visit came before Albion's first home game of the season - a 5-0 thrashing of Brighton. From left are Brendon Batson, Martin Jol, Ally Robertson and Romeo Zondervan. Albion had lost at Liverpool in their first away game.

Peter Eastoe, having scored in the slamming of Brighton, helps Albion to a second successive win with a cross-shot against a Manchester United side now under the management of Ron Atkinson. This made it 2-1 after Bryan Robson had drawn first blood for United, Albion going on to win 3-1. The keeper is Gary Bailey and the defender Kevin Moran while in the background is midfielder Romeo Zondervan.

Martin Jol looks on as Cyrille Regis swings his left foot to great effect to crash the first of Albion's goals past Derek Parkin and into the net in their 3-0 victory at Stoke in the early weeks of Ron Wylie's reign as manager. It was a third successive success for the side, secured by strikes on the break from Peter Eastoe and Alistair Brown. Regis hit a hat-trick in a win at Norwich a fortnight later.

Trouble ahead! Steve Sims drives a free-kick goalwards and Albion are on their way to a resounding 3-0 defeat on their first-ever competitive trip to Watford. No 7 Nigel Callaghan and no 11 John Barnes are the other members of Graham Taylor's newly-promoted side pictured while Cyrille Regis, Peter Eastoe, Martin Jol, Romeo Zondervan and Gary Owen are the Albion quintet.

Gary Owen, Paul Barron and Clive Whitehead keep guard in Albion's 1-0 top-flight home win over Aston Villa on October 2, 1982. Dennis Mortimer, later to serve as a Hawthorns coach, is disappointed to have arrived on the scene just too late. Nicky Cross scored the only goal for a side who had won five of their opening eight League games but who would catch a real cold by losing 6-1 in the League Cup at Nottingham Forest four days later.

Cyrille Regis looks on as Derek Statham aims a shot round David O'Leary in Albion's 2-0 defeat at Arsenal on October 16, 1982. The full-back was on as a substitute for his first senior appearance of an injury-ruined start to the season and missed only one more League game in 1982-83. Football's trying times were underlined by the fact that a crowd of only 21,000 were at Highbury to see Albion's run of three successive victories ended.

Regis again to the fore, this time with a clearing header at the expense of a corner during Albion's derby trip to Birmingham on November 6, 1982. But the relief of John Wile, Alistair Robertson, Martyn Bennett, Tony Godden and Derek Statham was only temporary. Blues won 2-1 despite a Peter Eastoe goal for a team who the previous weekend had caved in 6-1 at Ipswich in what proved to be the last of Brendon Batson's 220 games for the club.

Goal coming up for Albion as Romeo Zondervan applies the finishing touch to beat keeper Jim Arnold in a New Year's Day home game against Everton in 1983. Ex-Goodison forward Peter Eastoe is also on hand. This assured finish put Ron Wylie's side ahead but, despite a later strike by Gary Owen, they were pegged back in a 2-2 draw and their sequence without a League win would stretch to six matches before they overcame West Ham at The Hawthorns.

Asa Hartford returns to The Hawthorns to hold off Peter Eastoe and help Manchester City to a 2-0 League win on April 2, 1983. Garry Thompson had made a prolific start for the club with four goals in his first five games but Albion were on the slide. Having suffered eight consecutive defeats the previous spring, this was the second of six they lost in a row this time to again hover with the drop before winning three of their last four to finish in mid-table.

A famous Hawthorns landmark closed its doors for the last time in May, 1983 when brewers Mitchells and Butlers announced they were pulling out of the Throstle Club, leaving Albion supporters looking for an alternative watering hole, both on match-days and during the week. The facility was situated off the Birmingham Road behind the Rainbow Stand (the structure opposite the main stand) and has long since been wiped off the landscape.

Hands up if you've got full points! Garry Thompson (left) salutes his goal - made by the also-pictured Clive Whitehead - that put the seal on Albion's 2-0 home victory over Watford on October 1, 1983, and left keeper Steve Sherwood dejected. After losing their opening two games and conceding seven goals to Aston Villa and Stoke in the process, Albion were adjusting well to the summer exit of John Wile after his 619 appearances for the club. They won four of their next six games.

Johnny Giles was again Albion boss by the time of this 3-1 defeat against Arsenal on May 5, 1984. Despite an FA Cup defeat against Third Division Plymouth in his first game back, Giles steered a safe course to the season's end, keeping the club's heads above water, although 17th place was disappointing. Garry Thompson scored Albion's goal but is denied here by Pat Jennings, who made his 1,000th career appearance at the ground the previous season.

David Cross, first signed for Albion by Johnny Giles in 1977, was taken to The Hawthorns by him for the second time in the autumn of 1984. The striker was less than prolific in his new spell but, in the wake of Cyrille Regis being sold to Coventry, scored along with Garry Thompson in this 2-1 home win over Watford on December 8. Cross is on the prowl here with the grounded Thompson also doing his best to unsettle visiting keeper Tony Coton.

Carl Valentine cracks home the first of the goals that gave Albion a 2-0 lead at home to Arsenal on the last day of the 1984-85 campaign. Garry Thompson also netted, only for the Gunners to hit back with two goals in the last five minutes and salvage a point that left Albion in a final placing of 12th. Steve Hunt is no 4 while Nicky Cross is in the background beyond Kenny Sansom, the striker making the last of his 119 Baggies appearances before joining Walsall.

The calm before the fierce storm.....Alistair Robertson looks on as Clive Whitehead boots clear from John Trewick, by now in the colours of newly-promoted Oxford, on the opening day of 1985-86. The 1-1 Hawthorns draw, featuring debuts for goalscorer Imre Varadi and fellow striker Garth Crooks, was not a disaster for Albion but the follow-up was absolutely pitiful, the side conceding 30 goals in their next nine League games in a nightmare run relieved only by an odd-goal League Cup win over Port Vale.

Albion's 1985-86 woes started with this 2-0 midweek defeat away to Everton, with striker Adrian Heath beating a Martyn Bennett sliding challenge to slip a close-range shot past Tony Godden for one of his match-winning brace. It was the first of an Albion club record nine successive League defeats and one of 26 times the club would lose in that season's top flight. The trip to the reigning champions set the tone for one of the gloomiest campaigns in Hawthorns history.

Only 7,733 saw Albion take on Ipswich on September 7, 1985 - a depressing response to five successive First Division defeats in which no fewer than 16 goals were leaked. Despite this advance by Derek Statham (left) and goalscorer Garth Crooks, things didn't get any better against the East Anglians, who ran out 2-1 Hawthorns winners. Manchester United (5-1) and Coventry (3-0) then piled on the agony in the subsequent two matches and prompted manager Johnny Giles to resign before September was out.

Albion's only away League win of 1985-86 came on a snowy Sunday before just 11,514 fans at an equally downcast St Andrew's, where Martyn Bennett scored the only goal. The hero of the hour for the visitors, though, was Tony Godden, who denied Steve Whitton with this flying save and performed superbly. Brummie Steve Hunt (left) was playing the last of his 84 senior games for the club (20 goals) and joined Villa shortly afterwards. Albion and Blues were relegated by a distance, finishing bottom and bottom but one respectively.

Hurtling Downwards

With Albion back in Division Two for the first time in over a decade, only one of the first 11 League games of 1986-87 (home or away) attracted a crowd of more than 10,000. This Hawthorns clash with Huddersfield on the second Saturday of the season proved no great draw at the box office, although it had a happy ending after no 4 Martyn Bennett had scored and secured a second successive 1-0 victory. Stewart Evans (left) and Paul Dyson are the other celebrating players but the Ron Saunders era was a gloomy one.

Huddersfield are again the sufferers, this time on October 24, 1987. Tony Morley (centre) turns away after scoring the second goal of his hat-trick in a 3-2 victory at The Hawthorns, with Paul Dyson, a half-hidden Andy Gray and Bobby Williamson also showing their delight. Albion had finished a miserable 15th the previous season and, with the new campaign dawning on a similar note, Ron Saunders was quickly sacked and replaced by Ron Atkinson - the third manager to return to the club in the 1980s for a second spell in charge.

Left: New season, more change….Big Ron didn't last long second time round either and was gone shortly after this 1-1 draw at Plymouth on September 24, 1988. No 8 Don Goodman, who had scored the winner at Brighton four days earlier, looks on here as Carlton Palmer aims a looping header goalwards. Albion had survived the drop by a solitary point the previous spring and Atkinson was soon heading to Spain to manage Athletico Madrid.

Stuart Naylor takes the ball off the head of Wolves' Gary Bellamy but there was to be no happy ending for Albion in this resumption of Black Country derbies in October, 1989. Wolves won 2-1 in both this game and the return at Molineux before Albion bounced back to assume the upper hand in meetings with their biggest rivals.

Chris Kamara thunders a header past Stuart Naylor to open the scoring in Albion's 2-2 Second Division draw at Leeds in February, 1990, with Craig Shakespeare and no 10 Bernard McNally trying to cover. Goals at the other end by boyhood Leeds fan Don Goodman and Kevin Bartlett earned a point for an Albion side who were to finish 20th under Brian Talbot, waging a survival battle for the third time in four years. Picture courtesy of the Leeds Evening Post.

Gary Strodder yells his delight at scoring one of the six goals with which Albion thrashed Marlow in the opening round of the FA Cup in November, 1991. It was the second in a run of three victories for a side then managed by Bobby Gould but they went out of the Cup at Leyton Orient in the next round and also fell away in the race for promotion - a cue for Gould's departure amid some acrimony. Joining Strodder here is Bryan Robson's young brother Gary.

Daryl Burgess thrusts out a leg to halt Mansfield's Gary Castledine in Albion's 3-0 win at Field Mill on April 17, 1993. At the time, Ossie Ardiles' side were on their way to the play-offs in English football's third tier and secured their place by winning three and drawing one of their remaining four League matches. Brummie-born central defender Burgess made 377 senior Albion appearances between 1989 and 2001 and was given a testimonial by the club. Picture courtesy of the Nottingham Evening Post.

Climbing Back In Style

Albion made their fans sweat in 1992-93 before everything turned out fine. They lost 2-1 in the first leg of the play-off semi-final at Swansea after trailing 2-0 but turned the tables on a thrilling night at The Hawthorns in front of 26,025 three days later. Andy Hunt, whose partnership with Bob Taylor was a key factor behind their success, is on the ball above with Bernard McNally in close proximity, and lit the touchpaper by opening the scoring in the second leg. Ian Hamilton struck a beauty before half-time for goal no 2 to have Gary Strodder celebrating in front of the masses, the 3-2 aggregate win sending Albion to Wembley for the first time in 23 years.

Albion's final opponents were Port Vale, who beat Stockport in the other semi-final and also proved doughty opponents as the Wembley scoreline remained blank into the second half. But the Baggies were getting on top by the time Peter Swan was sent off for a professional tackle on Bob Taylor and the breakthrough came when Andy Hunt netted the rebound after this header by Gary Strodder had hit the post. Nicky Reid and Kevin Donovan completed a 3-0 victory and sparked ecstatic scenes among over 40,000 Albion fans at the stadium as well as among (from left) Ian Hamilton, Steve Lilwall, Strodder and Taylor. Albion ended the season with 114 goals in all competitions, Taylor's share standing at a magnificent 37 as part of a two-spell Hawthorns haul of 131 in 377 appearances.

FOREVER ALBION

Ossie Ardiles shocked Albion by walking out for Tottenham in the summer of 1993 - and the new Hawthorns season became little more than a grim struggle for survival in the higher league. That battle won, they laboured again in 1994-95, with this 1-0 home League win over Burnley on September 24 bringing them their first victory of the season - at the ninth try. It was secured by Bob Taylor's eagerly acclaimed goal but was something of a last hurrah in Keith Burkinshaw's 16-month reign as successor to Ardiles. The ex-Spurs manager lost his job after four subsequent defeats and was in turn replaced by Alan Buckley, who kept the club up comfortably despite a modest 19th place finish.

Andy Hunt finds his way to the ball blocked by Keith Curle in the Black Country derby at Molineux at the end of January, 1998. After Wolves' home-and-away double in 1996-97, this was revenge time for Denis Smith's men as they won with the only goal of the game from Hunt, a Curle own goal having given Albion - then managed by Ray Harford - maximum points by the same score at The Hawthorns four months earlier.

Richard Sneekes wheels towards the Birmingham Road End in celebration of one of the goals that beat already promoted Charlton 2-0 on the last day of the 1999-2000 season and kept Albion in the First Division at the expense of neighbours Walsall. Bob Taylor, recently re-signed by the club, also scored for a side who finished strongly with two wins and a draw in Gary Megson's first few weeks in charge.

Derek McInnes, clad in souvenir headgear, shakes hands with ref Eddie Wolstenholme following the infamous Battle of Bramall Lane on March 16, 2002. Albion were leading 3-0 when the game was abandoned several minutes early with hosts Sheffield United down to eight men after keeper Simon Tracey, former Albion man Georges Santos and Patrick Suffo had been sent off. A halt was called when the Blades also claimed two injuries that would have left them with barely half a team. Albion, inspired by some magnificent finishing underlined by McInnes' goal, threatened to walk off if ordered to replay the match but the result was allowed to stand.

Therace for the second automatic promotion spot behind Manchester City had become a straight Black Country sprint between Albion and Wolves by the time Igor Balis coolly converted this penalty at Bradford on April 13, 2002. It was one of the most vital spot-kicks in Baggies history, giving the side a last-gasp 1-0 victory and the knowledge that they would be up if they won their remaining game.

Top: Joy unlimited for Gary Megson as he joins in with the Birmingham Road End boing-boingers after Albion memorably secured promotion by beating Crystal Palace 2-0 on the last regular day of 2001-02. The Baggies knew they would be in the Premiership for the first time if they matched what Wolves did on the same day at Sheffield Wednesday. In the event, Wolves - 11 points clear of their arch-rivals at one stage - drew 2-2 and missed out in the play-offs as Birmingham went up instead. One of Megson's pre-match ploys was to have his players' families in the dressing-room as an extra gee-up.

Above: The second of the goals that beat Palace, scored by fans' idol Bob Taylor after Darren Moore had made the vital first breakthrough in the first half. The day climaxed an incredible 'roll.' Albion won seven and drew one of their last eight League games and were victorious in 13 of their final 17.

The prize for winning promotion: a first-day trip to Manchester United! Andy Johnson typifies a committed Albion display in their 1-0 defeat.

Albion went straight down again in the summer of 2003 with West Ham and wooden spoonists Sunderland. But they clearly had the promotion knack and bounced back at the first go, their rise confirmed by events elsewhere a few minutes before this 2-0 home win over Bradford on April 24. Geoff Horsfield is the man being congratulated on a goal here on a day when Lee Hughes (right) also scored.

Bryan Robson is feted as a hero after returning to Albion and leading them on a successful survival mission in 2004-05. It looked bleak when the man who had left The Hawthorns as a player almost a quarter of a century earlier succeeded Gary Megson in mid-November but Albion beat Portsmouth on the dramatic last afternoon of the season and so became the first club to survive in the Premiership after being bottom at Christmas. It's a memory guaranteed to have all Baggies fans wondering when the next major celebration will be.......

Subscribers

SCROLL OF HONOUR

Roger Adams

Malcolm Allsopp

Keith Archer

Nick Archer

Gary K Ashman

The Atkins Family

Scott Baggott

Jonathan Bagley

Stephen Bailey

Jon W Baldwin

The Bayley Family (Eddie, Rose, Stephen, Kate)

Steve, Karen, Hayley, Ellie

Ron Beards

Ronald Beardsmore

John Beetison

Michelle Bennett

Keith Bettam

Matt Bevan

George Blackham

Ian Blackham

Clive Blake

Dave Blewitt

Neil Blockley

Anthony and Michelle Blogg

Jay Boucher

Peter Bradbury

Robert S Bradley

Darren Bratt

Christopher Breakwell

David F Briers

Stuart Bullock

Alan James Bunn

Brian Burnet

Ann Burton

Chris Cadman

Sylvia and Terry Calloway

Alan Care

Steve Carr

Jamie and Ewan Carter

Ian M Cartwright

Kirsty Cherrington

Paul Cooke

Andrew John Cooper

Michael and William Corfield

The Cosnett Family (Lucy, Nicholas, Ashley, Christopher, Tracey)

Simon Cotter

Philip P Dale

Ken Dangerfield

Ilija Daniel

Richard Thomas Davenport

Trevor Frederick Davenport

Andrew Davies

Paul John Davies-Abingdon

Nigel Dennelly

D J Dickinson

SCROLL OF HONOUR

Andrew P Dodd

Marcus Dominick

Joe Eaton

Steve Eaton

Mark Eley

Simon L Elsmore

Stewart Evans

Betty Evitts

Paul Fenwick

Dorne Fereday

Henry Coley Fisher

Christopher John Foxall

Leslie Gee

Tony Gee

Graham Gibbons

Terry Gibbons

Ray Gibson

Arthur Goodall

James R Grainger

Terry Grainger

Daniel Green

Oliver Green

Stephen Green

David Greening

David Grigg

Sarah Rhian Guest

Kevin Hadley

Ben Hall

Dawn Hall

Geoff Hall

Robin H Harman

Christian Harmon

Marc Harris

Matthew D Hennefer

John Hewitt

Alistair Joseph Hickman

Cameron John Hickman

Geoff Hingley

Robert Hingley

Billy Hobbs

Stuart K Holliday

David Hollingmode

Nigel Holmes

Ian Robert Homer

John Homer

Rebecca Homer

Paul Horton

Ian Hoult

Jean, Barry, Clare, Nieve Hughes

Stuart Hunt

Nicholas Hynes

Jaden and Michael

Ron Jarratt

Bryn Johnson

SCROLL OF HONOUR

Dave Johnson

Alan Jones

Chris Jones

Ian Jones

Craig Robert Jones

Simon Joyce

James Keeley

Mike and Dorothy Kerry

Harmail Khela

Simon Khela

Sunil Khela

Richard Henry Kimberlee

John Edward King

Arthur Lakin

Graham Lawton

Harry Loynes

Bryan Lucas

Daniel MacDonald

Mick McCarthy

Gareth 'Macca' McDonald

Daniel McLaughlin

Mike

Robert L Mills

Ron Mills

Helen Moore

June Moore

Andy Morgan

Barry Moss

David Muir

Steve Mynott

Jack Nicholls

John R Nicholls

Roy Nicholls

Arthur Noble

Mike Phipps

Paul Plant

Alan Powell

Raymond Powell

Christopher Prinn

R C Pullin J.P.

Ronald William Randle

Jonathan Reid

Charlie Reynolds

Neil Reynolds

Daniel Richards

Nigel Riding

Graham Ridley

Christine Riley

Eric Roberts

Paul Roberts

David Neil Rogers

Shawn Rouke

SCROLL OF HONOUR

Jonathan Clive Round

Julian Rowe

Arthur Rushton

Carl Ruston

Archie Ryan

T R Saunders

Martin Scott

Mark E Selwood

Leah Shepherd

Barry Shermer

Neil Shingler

Colin Simpson

Dave Siviter

Mick Slevin

Hamid Smajic

Billy Paul Smith

Clive William Smith

Pat Smith

Stewart Smith

Steven Sorrill

David Spicer

Phillip Stanley

Philip Stevenson

David H Stokes

Stan Sunley

Patrick Talbot

Callum Taylor

David J Taylor

Scott Taylor

A W Thomas

M P Thomas

Michael Thomas

Sam Thompson

Matt Tisdale

Jonathan Tranter

Paul A Tranter

Brian Trevis

Jeremy Tromans

Mark Tromans

George Tubb

Kevin Tully

In memory of Frances Mary Turner

Peter Turner

Matt Tyler

Ben Upward

B P Walters

David Warner

Keith Wheeler

Derek Whitehouse

Geoffrey and Andrew Whitehouse

Kevin Whittingham

John L Williams

Paul N Williams

Stephen Williams

SCROLL OF HONOUR

Ian Withers	S R Wright
Brian Wood	
Martyn Woodward	Keith Young
Chelsea Wright	Steve Young

Other titles by Thomas Publications

(All written by David Instone unless otherwise stated)

The Bully Years (£8.99)

Wolves: Exclusive! (£6.99)

Sir Jack (£12.99)

Forever Wolves (£16.99)

When We Won the Cup (£15.99)

Running With Wolves by Peter Lansley (£16.99)

Le Tissier by Jeremy Butler (£14.99)

Wolves: The Glory Years (£16.99)

Forever Villa (£17.99)

All these books are available by writing to:
Thomas Publications
PO Box 17
Newport
Shropshire
TF10 7WT

by phoning:
07734 440095

or by emailing:
info@thomaspublications.co.uk

Further information about all of the above titles can be
obtained by logging on to our website:
www.thomaspublications.co.uk